GUIDE TO
THE APPALACHIAN TRAIL
IN
NORTH CAROLINA AND GEORGIA

(The Great Smoky Mountains National Park, Nantahala National
Forest, and Chattahoochee National Forest)

Revised Seventh Edition
Appalachian Trail Conference • Harpers Ferry • 1985

Field Editor:
  Margaret C. Drummond

Compilers of Data:
  Great Smoky Mountains National Park,
    Side Trails in the Smokies, and
    Nantahala National Forest, Sections 3-5 . . . . .James L. Botts
  Nantahala National Forest, Sections 6-10,
    and Side Trails in the Nantahalas . . . . .Barbara Lull
  Chattahoochee National Forest,
    Approaches to Springer Mtn., and
    Loop Hiking in Georgia . . . . .Margaret C. Drummond

Illustrators:
  Dory White, Georgia Appalachian Trail Club
  Sally Kesler, Nantahala Hiking Club
  Anne Lucio, ATC volunteer, Bradenton, Fla.

Maps:
  Richard B. Westlake

ISBN   0-917953-13-4

The insignia on the cover and title page represents the official marker of the
Appalachian Trail.

YES!
I WANT TO JOIN THE ATC

To: The Appalachian Trail Conference, Inc.
P.O. Box 807
Harpers Ferry, W. Va. 25425-0807

☐ My membership dues are enclosed. I understand my dues entitle me to all the benefits of membership, including five issues of *Appalachian Trailway News*, discounts on publications, and participation in ATC activities, and that the amount of my dues in excess of $15 is tax deductible. Please count me in as an:

☐ Individual member	$25	☐ Family	$30
☐ Member of A.T. club	$18	☐ Senior Citizen (65 or over)	$18
For discount, give name of A.T. club to which you belong		☐ Student (full time)	$18

Life:
  ☐ Individual $500
  ☐ Husband and Wife $750

_____

☐ I wish to make an additional, tax-deductible contribution in the following amount to help the ATC manage and protect the Appalachian Trail:

☐ $25   ☐ $50   ☐ $100   ☐ $500   ☐ $ _____

Name _____

Address _____

City _____ State _____ Zip _____

Phone (_____) _____

Optional Information

Age: _____

Occupation: _____

Outdoor Interests: _____

_____

_____

_____

Comments, Suggestions About This Guidebook:

_____

_____

_____

_____

_____

_____

_____

NOTICE TO ALL TRAIL USERS

The material contained in this guidebook has been supplied to the Conference by hiking clubs and individuals who maintain the Trail. The Conference representatives have not systematically verified the information. Although the Conference and the clubs strive for accuracy and thoroughness in the materials published, it is impossible to ensure that all the information published accurately describes the condition and location of the Trail. Consequently, the Conference and all member clubs and agents disclaim any liability for inaccuracies published in the guidebook.

The Trail crosses both private and public lands, the owners or administrators of which may alter Trail conditions and impose regulations on the use of the Trail. The Conference and all member clubs and agents expressly disclaim any liability for the negligence, wrongful actions, or omissions of any landowner with respect to the Trail.

This guide and associated maps refer to springs and streams as sources of water. The purity of water from unprotected water sources cannot be guaranteed and the ATC and all member clubs and agents expressly disclaim liability for any impurities in such water. Extreme care must be used in drinking such water. To be safe, all water should be purified by boiling or chemically treated before use.

Further, the Appalachian Trail Conference and all member clubs and agents expressly disclaim liability for the condition of the Trail, or for occurrences on it.

PREFACE

This seventh edition of *The Guide to the Appalachian Trail in North Carolina and Georgia* contains a generalized description and detailed Trail data for the Appalachian Trail from Davenport Gap, at the north end of the Great Smoky Mountains National Park, to Springer Mountain, Georgia, the southern terminus of the more than 2,100-mile-long Appalachian Trail, and includes side trails in the Great Smokies, the Nantahalas, and Georgia.

This volume represents the work of many people over many years. It builds on the labors of committees and collectors of Trail data who have provided material for four editions of the *Guide to the Appalachian Trail in the Southern Appalachians* and the previous six editions of this guide. The editor would like especially to recognize, and express appreciation for, the many years of dedicated work of Lionel Edney, of the Smoky Mountains Hiking Club; the Rev. A. Rufus Morgan, of the Nantahala Hiking Club; and Henry Morris, of the Georgia Appalachian Trail Club, Inc. These individuals pioneered and supplied carefully prepared Trail data from their respective sections for a period of many, many years. Although subsequent changes have been made, and new editors added, the work of these three still forms much of the material which the reader will find in this guide.

For this, the seventh edition, Trail data has been supplied by the following individuals: James L. Botts, of the Smoky Mountains Hiking Club and Appalachian Trail Conference Board of Managers, supplied material for the Great Smokies and for three northernmost sections of the Nantahala National Forest; Barbara Lull, of the Nantahala Hiking Club, researched and wrote the data for the Trail in the five southernmost sections of the Nantahala National Forest; Margaret Drummond, Georgia Appalachian Trail Club and member of the Appalachian Trail Conference Board of Managers, provided data for the Georgia section. Assistance of the Maps Committee and interested members of the GATC is also acknowledged. Other materials in this guide were written and reviewed by Margaret Drummond, field editor.

Constant changes take place along the Trail route. Those who observe such changes in approaches, accommodations, new trails, or anything that affects the data in the guide are requested to report such findings to the Publications Department, Appalachian Trail Conference, P.O. Box 807, Harpers Ferry, West Virginia 25425-0807.

ABBREVIATIONS

A.T. . . . . .Appalachian Trail
ATC . . . . .Appalachian Trail Conference
E . . . . .east
ft. . . . . .foot or feet
Ga. . . . . .Georgia
L . . . . left
mi. . . . . .mile or miles
Mt. . . . . .Mount
Mtn. . . . . .Mountain
N . . . . .north
N.C. . . . . .North Carolina
NE . . . . .northeast
NPS . . . . .National Park Service
NW . . . . .northwest
P.O. . . . . post office
R . . . . right
Rd. . . . . .road
S . . . . .Trail shelter or south
SE . . . . .southeast
St. . . . . street
SW . . . . .southwest
Tenn. . . . . .Tennessee
TVA . . . . .Tennessee Valley Authority
USFS . . . . .United States Forest Service
USGS . . . . .U.S. Geological Survey
W . . . . .west
yd. . . . . .yard or yards

TABLE OF CONTENTS

USE OF THE GUIDE AND TRAIL

Format of the Guidebook

An explanation of the format of this guide and of the theory on which it has been prepared may increase its usefulness and the reader's ease of access to desired information.

Appalachian Trail (A.T.) data are prepared in both directions so that the traveler may avoid the unsatisfactory necessity of having to reverse, mentally, Trail descriptions written for travel in an opposite direction. The description of the A.T. may always be read in the direction of travel.

The Trail data in this guide have been divided into 17 sections, separated by highway crossings in most cases. The data for each Trail section are divided into three parts. The first part includes general information needed primarily for planning. This material is arranged under individual headings in the following order and no attempt has been made to write this information for both directions:

> Brief Description of Section
> Points of Interest
> Road Approaches
> Maps
> Shelters, Campsites, and Water
> Public Accommodations and Supplies
> Precautions (if necessary)

Following this information is the detailed "Trail Description", the actual guide to the footpath. Data are given first for the hiker walking North to South on the Trail, and then for the hiker walking South to North. In this part of each section the reader will find a column of distances on the left. This gives the mileage from the start of the section to points of importance along the Trail section. At each mileage point (generally stream crossings, shelters, summits, important turns, etc.), the point itself is described, followed by directions on how the Trail goes to the next point.

When the traveler on the Trail finds that a marking is obliterated or the Trail is inadequately maintained, he should be able to refer to the detailed Trail description in the guide to orient himself, and thus be able to determine the route. The time and effort spent in checking may keep the hiker from missing the Trail completely. A.T. guides provide exact and detailed data to identify the Trail when the route is not obvious.

A major problem with guides is keeping the route descriptions up to date. Minor, or even major, Trail relocations occur. Timbering results in new roads, forest fires alter the landscape, floods may make former river crossings impassable, trees grow up in open summits, access roads are blocked, and shelters are built, moved, or become uninhabitable. There is constant change, both growth and decay, on many parts of the Trail.

Trail Marking

The entire A.T. is marked for travel in both directions. The marks are vertical white blazes, 2 inches wide and 6 inches long, on trees (or posts) and rocks. In some areas diamond-shaped A.T. metal markers will be found on trees.

Two blazes, one above the other, indicate a change in route or a warning to check blazes with care and to proceed with caution.

Normal procedure in marking the Trail is to position the blazes frequently enough to insure the safety of the hiker. In some cases where the Trail is less distinct, it may be possible to stand at one blaze and see the next. When the route is unmistakable, the blazes are less frequent. A hiker who has gone ¼ mile without seeing a blaze is advised to retrace his steps until he locates a blaze and is certain that no turn has been missed.

The Trail is blazed for walking in both directions. If no blaze is visible on what seems to be the route ahead, a glance backwards may locate blazes for travel in the opposite direction and reassure the hiker that he is still on the Trail.

Side trails from the A.T. to water, viewpoints, and shelters will usually be blazed in blue. Intersecting trails, not part of the A.T., may be blazed in a variety of colors.

The Southern Appalachians

The southern Appalachian Mountains are the highest and are considered by some to be the most rugged of the entire Appalachian chain. Except perhaps for those in Maine, they represent the superlative in the "wilderness" and the "primitive" areas made accessible by the A.T. Much of the route is ridgecrest travel and much is above 5,000 ft. elevation. The views often consist of a vast sea of lofty mountain ranges in all directions.

Travelers from other sections of the A.T. will find much contrast here. With increasing elevation, particularly in the Great Smokies, the flora become similar to that found farther north. Southern Appalachian ''balds'', great unforested summits comparable to the glaciated heights of New England, afford magnificent views.

Apart from the endless ridges, perhaps the most impressive feature of the Trail in the southern Appalachians is the profusion of flowering shrubs, rhododenron, azalea, and laurel. In full bloom their dense masses and ''thickets'' make the hiker's path one of almost indescribable beauty. The floral display reaches its height in late June and July. Elevation influences the blooming season, and on the summits the display occurs much later than in the valleys.

The Trail hiker will encounter an unusual variety of trees here. The Great Smoky Mountains National Park, alone, contains more species than the European continent. *The Appalachians,* a book by Maurice Brooks (Houghton Mifflin Co., Boston, 1965), vividly describes the Trail and its environment.

3

The Trail route covered by this guide also contrasts with sections farther north in that most of it is publicly owned. Most of it lies in the Great Smoky Mountains National Park and the two National Forests, the Nantahala in North Carolina, and the Chattahoochee in Georgia. Such public ownership results in protection under the National Trails System Act and insures the preservation of the primitive aspects of the Trail environment. Further purchases of land will increase the publicly owned areas. The completion of this acquisition program will result in a continuous public domain for those who walk and camp.

Within the National Forests much of the Trail is graded and avoids steep ascents and descents. It bypasses many summits from which there are no views in the summertime. As a rule this type of Trail affords easier walking than that which closely follows the ridgecrest. The graded Trail built by the NPS in the eastern Smokies from Davenport Gap to Clingmans Dome (38 miles) is wider, has easier grades, and is more obviously constructed than USFS trails. Contrasting with the graded Trail in the eastern Smokies, the 26-mile stretch of Trail from Clingmans Dome to Shuckstack Mtn., above the Little Tennessee River, has an unworked footway for most of the distance.

The Trail in the southern Appalachians provides mostly off-road travel, except for short distances on country roads. It is constructed for, and intended for foot travel except in parts of the Great Smokies where horses are permitted. Use of motorized vehicles is expressly prohibited on the A.T. under the National Trails System Act.

Trail Route

A study of Arnold Guyot's 1863 manuscript, "Notes on the Geography of the Mountain District of Western North Carolina", reveals that the southern Appalachians east of the Tennessee Valley and Cumberland Mtns. form an enormous oval, extending from southern Virginia to northern Georgia and connected by high parallel transverse ridges. The Appalachian Trail utilizes portions of both forks and a connecting transverse ridge, the Nantahala Mtns. The section described in this guide between Big Pigeon and Little Tennessee Rivers is what Arnold Guyot called the "master chain" of the southern Appalachians. All but a short distance of it is included in the Great Smoky Mountains National Park. Its terrain is the highest, wildest, and most primitive of the entire Appalachian Range.

The Great Smokies section terminates at the Little Tennessee River (Fontana Dam). After including the magnificence of the Great Smokies, the route turns back towards the Blue Ridge, the east fork of the oval. It leaves the crest of the Great Smokies at Doe Knob, crosses the Little Tennessee River at Fontana Dam, and climbs to the summit of Yellow Creek Mtn. Beyond, the route leads east.

A difficult 28-mile section of Trail goes through the Yellow Creek-Wauchecha-Cheoah Range. At the Nantahala River the route turns south. Here begins a Forest Service Trail through a 55-mile region, a worthy peer of the Great Smokies. The Nantahalas are a land of 5,000-ft. peaks and 4,000-ft. gaps through an unbroken expanse of mountain ranges. In addition to Wesser and Wayah Balds, Standing Indian, the "Grandstand of the Southern Appalachians", is the dominating feature of this area. The 21-mile walk from Wallace Gap to Deep Gap over Standing Indian has few equals on the A.T.

For the 79 miles in the Chattahoochee National Forest in northern Georgia, the high elevation and ruggedness of the Trail are maintained. On Blood Mtn., only 30 miles from the southern terminus, the Trail is still over 4,400 ft. high. The two forks of the oval of the southern Appalachians meet at Springer Mtn., the southern terminus of the Appalachian Trail.

Maintenance of the Trail

Although responsibility for National Scenic Trails, including the Appalachian Trail, is vested by the 1968 National Trails System Act in the U.S. Departments of Interior (NPS) and Agriculture (USFS), the work of maintaining the Trail, keeping it open and blazed, is done largely by volunteers. The volunteers who maintain sections of the A.T. covered by this guide are members of A.T. maintaining clubs — the Smoky Mountains Hiking Club, the Nantahala Hiking Club, and the Georgia Appalachian Trail Club, Inc. These volunteers are not paid and may be seen by hikers, usually on weekends, as they cut weeds, saw blowdowns, install water bars, and repair shelters. Sometimes Trail maintenance is done by club members on an official club outing. In other cases, short sections of the A.T., are assigned to club members for individual maintenance. Some clubs call these members ''section overseers'' or ''section maintainers''.

Volunteers welcome assistance from hikers. Hikers sometimes stop to help with the ongoing project. However, at all times, hikers can help by carrying out the litter left by others, protecting water sources, showing concern for shelters, signs, and other structures, and by not cutting across switchbacks. Any hiker wishing to become involved in Trail maintenance is invited to contact a local A.T. maintaining club.

Great Smoky Mountains National Park

Between Davenport Gap and the Little Tennessee River, the A.T. is entirely within the Great Smoky Mountains National Park. The Park is in both Tennessee and North Carolina and the Trail follows the ridgetops along the state lines. Park District Ranger offices are in Bryson City, N.C., and Gatlinburg, Tenn. The main park headquarters is in Gatlinburg.

National Forests

In North Carolina, the Trail lies mostly within the Nantahala National Forest. The Supervisor's office is at 50 S. French Broad Ave., Box 2750, Asheville, N.C. 28802. In Georgia, the entire Trail is within the boundaries of the Chattahoochee National Forest. The Supervisor's office is at 508 Oak St., NW, Gainesville, Ga. 30501.

Maps of the Trail Route

The Tennessee Valley Authority (TVA), since 1953, has carried out an extensive mapping program with the U.S. Geological Survey (USGS).

The entire Trail route in the area covered by this guide is mapped on contoured quadrangles, all in 7½ minute series (about 0.4 mi. = 1 in.). Each section of the guide lists the specific maps which cover that part of the Trail.

Quadrangles may be obtained from the Branch of Distributing, USGS, 1200 South Eads St., Arlington, Va. 22202, and from Map Sales, TVA, 400 W. Summit Hill Dr., Knoxville, Tenn. 37902. The price at the time of this publication was $2.50 + mailing per map. An area map for each state showing all the quadrangles and listing other maps may be obtained from USGS.

The USFS, Chattahoochee National Forest, publishes a map referred to in the guide as the USFS Chattahoochee National Forest Map. This map shows the Trail, road accesses, campgrounds, etc. This recreational map may be obtained from the Forest Supervisor's office, 508 Oak St., NW, Gainsville, Ga. 30501. A similar map of the Nantahala National Forest is available from the Asheville office (50 S. French Broad Ave., Box 2750, Asheville, N.C. 28802).

The Hiker's Responsibilities

In Georgia, the Trail is entirely on public lands. In North Carolina it is on private lands in some locations. In many cases a relationship of trust and mutual respect has existed for many years between these landowners and the maintaining club(s). It is the hiker's responsibility not to betray that trust and to do nothing that would affront or concern the landowners, such as building fires where they are prohibited, vandalizing, littering, camping where it is not permitted, etc. A landowner's reaction to these transgressions may be to close the Trail route across his property and thus threaten the continuity of the Trail.

Dogs are permitted in National Forests but only on leashes. This restriction is for good reasons. Dogs annoy some hikers and campers and they chase wildlife. They often get lost and do not survive.

Hikers should always stay on the Trail. In many places switchbacks are close together and eager hikers, seeing the route ahead, leave the Trail, and bushwhack straight uphill or downhill. This is a practice that often destroys the environment. A straight trail uphill or downhill in the South, where the annual rainfall is high, can become a river during a downpour. Rain will erode such steep trails.

Shelters

There is a continuous chain of shelters spaced about 3-14 miles apart throughout the section of A.T. covered by this guide. Each section of this guide lists the shelters in the introductory information and the distances to the shelter from the start of the Trail section is given in the Trail Description.

All of the shelters on this section of the A.T. were built after 1937. With few exceptions, they were constructed by the NPS or the USFS. They are well built and afford protection from rain, an essential in the southern Appalachians.

Shelters are three-sided and have open fronts. They may be fitted with bunks or have a wooden floor that serves as a sleeping platform. Usually nearby are a spring, and sometimes a toilet, fireplace, tables, and benches. The hiker should bring cooking utensils and a small stove.

Sometimes these structures are called by different names in different areas: ''lean-tos'', ''shelters'' or ''shelter cabins'', and ''Trail shelters''. This guide uses the word shelter when referring to most of these structures.

These facilities are provided primarily for the long distance hiker who may have no other means of shelter. Persons planning short overnight hikes, who may have access to and from the Trail from road crossings of the Trail, are asked to consider this and carry tents. This is a good practice anyway since the Trail is heavily used and shelters are usually crowded during the summer months. Camps and other organizations are asked to keep their groups small (six to eight people, plus leaders). They should carry tents and not monopolize shelters. Although a shelter is available on a "first-come, first-served" basis, everyone is asked to cooperate and consider the needs of others who may have planned to use the shelter.

Fires

Fires are an ever-present danger on the A.T. and in the forests. Hikers should build fires only within a fire-ring, keep the fires small and dowse them before leaving. It is wise for the hiker to carry a small stove.

In building fires, hikers should be conservative in their use of wood and careful of where it is collected. Many campsites suffer visible deterioration from hikers who cut wood from trees within the campsite. Only dead and down wood should be used for fires, and etiquette dictates that a supply be left for the next hiker, especially if the wood used came from a stored supply.

Water

Water sources may be springs or streams. The hiker is cautioned that regardless of the remoteness of the site, the water may be unsafe and should be treated before drinking. The purity of an unprotected water source cannot be guaranteed.

It is the hiker's responsibility not to contaminate a water supply or the surrounding area. All washing of dishes, clothes, and hands should be done well away from, and on the lower side of, a stream. It is handy for the hiker to carry a collapsible basin in order to collect water at the stream and to carry it to a remote site for washing.

Advice and Precautions

Long distance hikes on the A.T. should be undertaken only after considerable study and preparation as to physical condition, equipment, and knowledge of possible problems and how to avoid them. The ruggedness of the terrain and the exertion required to travel it should not be underestimated.

Getting Lost

The Trail hiker who uses the A.T. for more than day-hiking needs a thorough understanding of the Trail.

The Trail often has long sections where there are few opportunities for orientation or checking the route. The traveler should not proceed more than a quarter of a mile at the most (roughly five minutes of hiking) without noticing some Trail marking. If none is found in this interval, it is advisable to retrace the course until some indisputable indication of the Trail appears. The Trail should then be carefully checked to determine the error.

The cardinal mistake, and the basis for many unfortunate experiences, is an insistence on going forward when the route seems obscure or dubious. Haste, such as in a desire to avoid darkness to reach camp, only complicates the difficulty. When in doubt, it is wise to remain at the point of difficulty, since this prevents straying farther from the route. A night out close to the Trail is much better than being genuinely lost.

Hiking long distances alone is not recommended. A lone hiker who suffers a serious accident or illness may risk his life if he has not made some contingency plans. If a long-distance hiker persists on traveling alone, the destination and estimated time of arrival should be known to someone who will initiate inquiries or search if the hiker does not return when expected. It is wise to report plans and progress every few days.

A lone hiker who has lost his way and chooses to bushwhack toward evidence of human habitation generally risks danger of accident. If he falls, he may not be discovered for days or even weeks. The general advice to all lone hikers is to stay on the Trail (or at least a trail) even if it means spending an unplanned night in the woods. A pack should always contain enough food and water to sustain a hiker until daylight, when a careful retracing of his steps may lead him with ease back to a safe route.

Most of the Trail is used enough that a person who cannot walk because of an injury can reasonably expect to be found. However, if the area is remote and the weather bad, few hikers will be on the Trail. In this case, it is best to study the guide to locate the nearest point on the Trail where people are likely to be and to make an attempt to move in that direction, however slowly.

If it is necessary to leave a heavy pack behind, the hiker should be certain to carry with him the essentials he will need if rescue is delayed. If the weather is bad, a night in the open without proper covering could be very dangerous.

Trail Relocations

In connection with Trail conditions, particular note should be made of the Appalachian Trail Conference's publication, *Appalachian Trailway News* (published five times annually). While this publication is not intended as a guidebook supplement, major relocation information appears regularly. The publication is, therefore, of much value to users of the A.T. Subscription to the *Appalachian Trailway News* also affords, in a small way, support to the entire Trail project. (See address on back of title page, and membership application.)

Hikers should always follow the marked Trail. If it differs from the Trail description in the guidebook, this is usually because a relocation has recently been made. The Trail was probably relocated to avoid some hazard or undesirable feature, or to take it off private property. If hikers use the old Trail, they may be trespassing and thus generating ill will toward themselves and other Trail hikers.

Compass Deviation

The compass deviation in this section is small (about 1°) and is westerly. To change the compass course to the true geographical course, the amount of variation is applied to the left; that is, subtracted. In determining the compass course from the true geographical course, the amount of deviation is applied to the right; that is, added.

Weather

The liklihood of heavy, prolonged rainstorms in the South should be fully understood. Rain gear (full length ponchos, cagoule, or rain suit), a waterproof tent, and small cooking stove are essentials for extended hiking in this area. Waterproof matches and a change of clothing are also necessary.

Face, shoulders, and legs should be protected from sunburn. Shorts should be worn with caution.

On the balds it may be cold, rainy, and windy at any time of the year. Hikers should be well prepared with warm clothing, sleeping gear, and tents.

Some of the Trail covered by this guide is at elevations of over 5,000 ft. For this reason, winter condtions correspond to Trail sections much farther north.

Wind will reduce the air temperature by 1° (degree) to 2° F. for each mile per hour of its speed. For example, a wind of 20 miles per hour at 30° F. will reduce the equivalent temperature to about 3° F!

Parking

Travelers are cautioned not to leave automobiles unattended overnight in remote areas, because of the possibility of vandalism. It is wise to leave vehicles near a house or building after obtaining permission from the owner.

Pests

Poisonous snakes (rattlesnakes and copperheads) may be encountered A suction-type snake-bite kit should be carried.

Black flies, prevalent in the North, are not found in the southern Appalachians. Some annoyance may be encountered from chiggers, no-see-ums, mosquitoes, and other insects which abound in summer. Therefore, a hiker should carry a suitable repellent.

The necessity for protecting food from bears, especially in the Great Smokies, is discussed in the introduction to the chapter on the Great Smokies.

Poison Ivy

Poison Ivy, a vine with leaves in alternating clusters of three, is prolific in the South. The hikers, especially if wearing shorts, should exercise caution. The vine is often on trees and fences but may also be low growing or trailing on the ground. In winter, touching even the bare stems of the plant, can cause an allergic reaction in people who are sensitive to it.

Distress Signals

An emergency call for distress consists of three short calls, audible or visible, repeated at regular internals. A whistle is particularly good for audible signals. Visible signals may include, in daytime, light flashed with a mirror or smoke puffs or, at night, a flashlight or three small bright fires.

Anyone recognizing such signals should acknowledge it by a signal of two calls. He should then go to the distressed and determine the nature of the emergency. If more competent aid is needed, he should try to arrange for it.

Alice laughed. 'There's no use trying,' she said, 'one can't believe impossible things.'

'I daresay you haven't had much practice,' said the Queen. 'When I was younger, I always did it for half an hour a day. Why, sometimes I've believed as many as six impossible things before breakfast.'

LEWIS CARROLL
Through the Looking Glass

First Aid

First aid is a difficult subject to cover adequately in the space that can be devoted to it in a guidebook. Other publications, such as the *Red Cross First Aid Manual,* are readily available and do it well. This guide deals with the subject in outline form only.

First, proper preparation for a hiking trip will greatly reduce the likelihood of an accident or other situations requiring the need for first aid. Second, some training in first aid is very desirable, especially for the trip leader. Training should cover the following:

1. Severe bleeding
2. Shock
3. Bone fractures
4. Sprains
5. Blisters
6. Neck and back injuries
7. Dislocations
8. Frostbite
9. Hypothermia
10. Sunburn
11. Heat weakness, cramps, and exhaustion
12. Snakebite
13. Artificial respiration
14. Heat stroke and sun stroke

THE APPALACHIAN TRAIL

The Appalachian Trail (A.T.) is a continuous, marked footpath extending from Katahdin, a granite monolith in the central Maine wilderness, some 2,100 miles south to Springer Mountain in Georgia. It is a skyliner route along the crest of the ranges generally referred to as "Appalachian," hence the name of the Trail.

The A.T. traverses 14 states; Virginia has the longest section with about 500 miles, approximately one-fourth of the total. West Virginia has the shortest section, with some 20 miles along the Virginia-West Virginia boundary. The greatest elevation along the Trail route is on Clingmans Dome in the Great Smokies, 6,643 feet. The Trail is only slightly above sea level at its crossing of the Hudson River in New York.

The Appalachian Trail Conference

The Appalachian Trail Conference (ATC) is a volunteer, nonprofit corporation dedicated to the maintenance and preservation of the A.T. It coordinates the efforts of Trail clubs, state and local governments, federal land management agencies, and individuals in Trail management and maintenance.

The ATC publishes booklets and supplies information on construction and maintenance of hiking trails, guidebooks for all sections of the A.T., and general information on hiking and trail use in general. The Conference's headquarters is located in Harpers Ferry, West Virginia. The mailing address is Appalachian Trail Conference, P.O. Box 807, Harpers Ferry, W.Va. 25425-0807 (phone (304) 535-6331). Office hours are 9 a.m. to 5 p.m. weekdays.

The Trail route is divided into three regions: New England, Mid-Atlantic, and Southern. The affairs of the Conference are managed by a Board of Managers consisting of a Chairman, 3 Vice Chairmen, a Treasurer, a Secretary, a Corresponding Secretary, and 18 persons, 6 from each of the three regions. ATC general sessions are held every second or third year.

The membership of the Conference consists of organizations which maintain the Trail or contribute to the Trail project, individuals who in either personal or official capacity are responsible for the maintenance of sections of the Trail, and individual dues-paying members.

ATC membership includes a subscription to *Appalachian Trailway News,* published in March, May, July, September, and November. The

Conference also issues a newsletter, *The Register,* written for Trail maintainers, as well as bulletins and guidebooks. Membership application material and a complete list of publications with current prices are available from the ATC by writing to the address above.

History of the Trail

Credit for the establishment of the A.T. belongs to three leaders and countless volunteer workers. The first proposal for the Trail to appear in print was an article by Benton MacKaye of Shirley, Massachusetts, "The Appalachian Trail, an Experiment in Regional Planning," in the October 1921 issue of the *Journal of American Institute of Architects.*

MacKaye's challenging idea kindled considerable interest, but at the time the only outdoor organizations that could participate in the creation of the Trail were almost entirely east of the Hudson River, and there were only four existing trail systems that could be incorporated into it. The Appalachian Mountain Club (AMC) maintained an excellent series of trails in New England. However, most of the trails ran north-south; the Trail could not cross New Hampshire until the chain of huts built and operated by the AMC permitted an east-west alignment. In Vermont the southern 100 miles of the Long Trail, then being developed in the Green Mountains, was connected to the White Mountains by the trails of the Dartmouth Outing Club.

West of the Hudson there were few trails, even in the Harriman-Bear Mountain section of Palisades Interstate Park. However, it was here that the first section of the A.T. was built in 1922 by a number of hiking clubs of the area that later affiliated into the New York-New Jersey Trail Conference.

Although interest spread to Pennsylvania and to New England, little additional work was done until 1926, when Arthur Perkins of Hartford, Connecticut, took on the task of persuading various groups to locate and cut the footpath in the wilderness. His enthusiasm provided the momentum that carried the Trail to its conclusion.

It was Judge Perkins who interested Myron H. Avery of Lubec, Maine, and Washington, D.C., in the Trail. Avery, as chairman of the ATC from 1931 to 1952, enlisted the aid and coordinated the work of the hundreds of men and women whose work brought the Trail to its completion in 1937, when the last link (on the north slope of Spaulding Mtn., Maine) was opened on August 14. In the southern states there were few trails and even fewer clubs. The skyline route now followed by the A.T. was developed largely within National Forests, and a number of clubs formed in various parts of the southern Appalachians have taken responsibility for much of the Trail.

Since the Trail was made continuous, the encroachments of highways, housing developments, summer resorts, and the like have caused many relocations, and the problem of maintaining the wilderness character of the Trail has become more and more severe.

At the Eighth Appalachian Trail Conference held in June 1937 in the Great Smoky Mountains National Park, ATC member Edward B. Ballard proposed to the Conference a plan for an ''Appalachian Trailway,'' which would set apart an area on each side of the Trail and dedicate it to the interests of those who travel on foot. This plan was adopted by the Conference, and steps were taken to carry into effect this long-range program to ensure the perpetuation and protection of the A.T. These efforts culminated in the execution on October 15, 1938, of an agreement between NPS and USFS for the promotion of the Appalachian Trailway. Thus there was created a new type of recreational area to be known as the Appalachian Trailway, a zone extending through the National Parks and Forests for a distance of 1 mile on each side of the A.T. Within this zone there were to be no new paralleling roads for motor transportation or any other incompatible developments. There was to be no timber cutting within 200 feet of the Trail. A similar agreement, creating a zone ¼ mile in width, was entered into with the states through which the Trail passes.

Protection of the A.T. was expanded under the National Trails System Act of 1968. Under it, a national system of trails was established, and as initial components the Appalachian Trail and the Pacific Crest Trail were designated National Scenic Trails. The act provides that the Secretary of the Interior, in consultation with the Secretary of Agriculture, will administer the A.T., primarily as a footpath, and protect the Trail against incompatible activities and the use of motorized vehicles. Provision is also made for acquisition of rights-of-way for the Trail both inside and outside the boundaries of federally administered areas, by easement, purchase, exchange, or, as a last resort, condemnation.

In 1970 the Act was implemented by supplemental agreements among the NPS, the USFS, and the ATC. These agreements established the

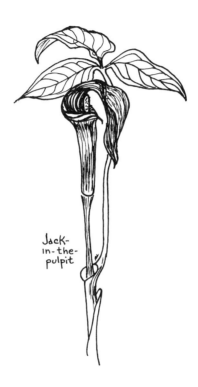

Jack-
in-the-
pulpit

specific responsibilities of these three organizations for the initial mapping, selection of right-of-way, relocations, maintenance, development, acquisition of land, and protection of the Trail. Agreements were also made between the NPS and the various states through which the Trail passes. These agreements encourage states to acquire and protect the right-of-way for the Trail outside of federally owned land.

Slow progress of federal protection efforts and the lack of initiative of some states led Congress in 1978 to amend the National Trails System Act. The amendment, referred to as the Appalachian Trail Bill, represented the collective efforts of a dedicated group of volunteers, federal officials, and concerned citizens. President Carter signed the legislation on March 21, 1978.

The new legislation left the purpose of the original act unchanged, but emphasized the need to proceed quickly with the protection of the A.T., including the acquisition of a Trail corridor. For this purpose Congress authorized an expenditure of 90 million dollars and established a three-year deadline for the substantial completion of the protection program. In addition, the amendment requires that certain plans and progress reports be prepared and submitted for congressional review.

The program resulting from the amendment is presently being implemented as a combined effort of the NPS and the Trail clubs under the leadership of the ATC, with the aid and cooperation of the USFS and various state and local agencies. In several states similar, yet separate, programs are progressing concurrently with the federal program. During the process, and following its completion, ATC and the Trail clubs will continue to retain the primary responsibility for maintenance and management of the Trail.

For additional information on the A.T., the hiker should consult the following:

- *Campfires Along the Appalachian Trail*. Raymond Baker, New York, Carlton Press. 1971. 120 p.
- *The Appalachian Trail*. Ronald M. Fisher, Washington, National Geographic Society. 1972. 199 p.
- *Appalachian Hiker II*. Edward B. Garvey, Oakton, Va., Appalachian Books. 1978. 429 p.
- *The Appalachian Trail: Wilderness on the Doorstep*. Ann and Myron Sutton, Philadelphia, J.B. Lippincott. 1967. 180 p.
- *Hiking the Appalachian Trail,* edited by James R. Hare, Emmaus, Pennsylvania, Rodale Press. 1975. 2 vols. 2,009 p.
- *The Appalachians*. Maurice Brooks, Boston, Riverside Press. 1965. 346 p.

THE TRAIL IN THE GREAT SMOKY MOUNTAINS NATIONAL PARK

Distance 68.6 miles

Great Smoky Mountains National Park

The 68.6 miles of the A.T. between the Pigeon River and the Little Tennessee River lie almost entirely within Great Smoky Mtns. National Park along the crest of the Great Smokies — the master chain of the southern Appalachians. With the exception of the Black Mtns. in N.C., they are the loftiest and most rugged in the East. The trails within the Park were constructed and are maintained by the National Park Service (NPS). The A.T. in the Park is managed cooperatively by the NPS and the Smoky Mountains Hiking Club based in Knoxville, Tenn.

Although the first serious proposal to establish a national park in the Smoky Mtns. was made before 1900, the efforts that were ultimately successful began in 1923. Private and public efforts to acquire land began in 1925. In 1928 John D. Rockefeller, Jr., contributed five million dollars to match contributions of states and private citizens, and purchase of land began in earnest. By 1930, 158,000 acres had been bought, and by 1935, 400,000 acres. The Park was formally dedicated in 1940 by President Franklin D. Roosevelt.

An adequate portrayal of the attractions of Great Smoky Mtns. National Park is beyond the scope of this chapter. Visitors will find information in the NPS leaflet that may be procured from the Park office.

Among the best of currently available books on the Great Smoky Mtns. are:

- *Birth of a National Park*. Carlos C. Campbell. University of Tennessee Press, Knoxville, Tenn. 1960.
- *The Great Smoky Mountains*. Laura Thornborough. University of Tennessee Press, Knoxville, Tenn. 1963.
- *Our Southern Highlanders*. Horace Kephart. Macmillan, New York. 1963. Written in 1913; revised in 1922.
- *Strangers in High Places*. Michael Frome. Doubleday & Co., Garden City, N.Y. 1966.

Other Trails in the Smokies

There have been, from time to time, several guidebooks on the Great Smokies. One of these publications, *The Smokies Guide,* by George M Stephens (Stephens Press, Box 5655, Asheville, N.C. 28803; $2.50) gives a comprehensive and readable account of the Park but emphasizes the region rather than its trail system.

A folder entitled *100 Favorite Trails of the Great Smokies and Carolina Blue Ridge,* complete with map and description of each, is also available ($1) from Stephens Press. *Hiking in the Great Smokies,* by Carson Brewer (65 pp.; $1), may be obtained from the Great Smoky Mountains Natural History Association, Park Headquarters, Gatlinburg, Tenn. 37738.

The most comprehensive publication on trails in the Great Smokies is *Hiker's Guide to the Smokies* by Dick Murlless and Constance Stallings. published by the Sierra Club in 1973. This 375-page Sierra Club Totebook gives detailed descriptions of more than 500 trails in the Park, plus accessory information on park history, geology, flora and fauna, and regulations.

More information may be obtained from the Park Service headquarters at Gatlinburg, Tenn., and from the Smoky Mountains Hiking Club, Box 1454, Knoxville, Tenn. 37901.

Maps

The map in this guide depicts the part of the Park through which the A.T. passes. For detailed topography, see the following 7½-minute quadrangles: USGS Waterville, Tenn.-N.C.; Hartford, Tenn.-N.C.; Luftee Knob, N.C.-Tenn.; Mt. Guyot, Tenn.-N.C.; Mt. LeConte, Tenn.-N.C.; Clingmans Dome, N.C.-Tenn.; Silers Bald, N.C.-Tenn.; Thunderhead Mtn., N.C.-Tenn.; Cades Cove, Tenn.-N.C.; and Fontana Dam, N.C. These maps are obtainable for $2.50 each + mailing from Branch of Distribution, U.S. Geological Survey, 1200 South Eads Street, Arlington, Va. 22202, or from Map Sales, Tennessee Valley Authority, 400 W. Summit Hill Drive, Knoxville, Tenn. 37902. Also available ($4 each + mailing) are the following maps for the Great Smokies: Great Smoky Mountains National Park (East Half) and Great Smoky Mountains National Park (West Half) — scale 1:62,5000, or approximately 1 mi. to 1 in.; contour interval, 50 ft.; size of each 28 x 36 in. These cover the Park and adjacent area (2,730 square mi.) and show all roads and trails in existence at the time of its last revision, 1972.

Campfires

Firewood is so scarce in the Smokies that hikers are advised to carry gasoline stoves. Stoves have added advantage of providing cooking facilities in wet weather, which frequently occurs in the Smokies.

Water

A canteen, preferably two, is indispensable. Sources of water have been indicated in the data. In dry seasons, it is often necessary at many of the springs to go farther down the mountain. Water may also be located on the slopes of other gaps in addition to those specifically mentioned.

Bears

The protection afforded to all forms of wildlife within the Great Smoky Mtns. National Park has resulted in a problem akin to that experienced in the western parks — damage and depredation by bears.

Bears are particularly numerous at parking places and are attracted by food at shelters and in pits. The problem would be minimized if everyone obeyed the rule not to feed bears or to leave food at shelters where bears can get it. Bears will steal food if it is not protected. Most shelters in the Park have wire grills across the open front so that food may be safely stored in them. Some have separate food caches. If such storage places are not available, hikers should suspend their food and packs from a rope or wire stretched high between two trees. Food left in automobiles may attract bears and result in damage to the car. Packs and tents may be similarly damaged. Excess food should be burned or carried out, not buried or left in the open. Tin cans and other things that will not burn should also be carried out. All Trail travelers should avoid attracting bears to parking places and shelters by not leaving food where bears can get it. Hikers should give bears a wide berth, particularly if they have cubs with them. It is dangerous to feed, tease, frighten, or molest them in any way.

Pets and firearms are not permitted in the Park.

Flora

As far as the preferable season for travel is concerned, the flora, which is an outstanding feature of the southern Appalachians, shows to best advantage in June and July when the rhododendron and azaleas are in bloom. The display of flame azalea is particularly outstanding. At this season, however, there is greater likelihood of wet weather.

Shelters

There is a chain of 13 shelters along the A.T. in the Park, five in the eastern part and eight in the western part. These shelters were specially built by the NPS for use on the Trail, and they are located at intervals of an easy day's travel. Use of each structure is limited to one night. Garbage pits at shelters have been filled in by the NPS, and users are expected to carry out all nonburnable refuse. Shelters on each section of Trail in the Park are listed in the introduction to that section.

Camping Permits

Permits are required by the NPS for both camping and use of the shelters and approved campsites along the A.T. This is not a requirement on most other parts of the Trail. It is a violation of Park Service regulations, punishable by fine, for overnight hikers to travel in the Great Smoky Mtns. National Park without a camping permit. A.T. shelter permits for through-hikers may be obtained at ranger stations and visitor centers in the Park or at the USFS French Broad Ranger District Headquarters in Hot Springs, N.C., which is located across from the post office on the main street in town. Northbound through-hikers may get permits at the TVA Fontana Dam visitor center.

In 1972, in an attempt to prevent gross overcrowding at shelters and the deterioration of the Trail environment, the Park Service began a system of issuing for a given night only as many camping permits as the capacity of the shelter. Camping adjacent to the shelters as well as at unauthorized places along the trails is forbidden. Hikers planning trips of more than one day should write to Great Smoky Mountains National Park, Gatlinburg, Tenn. 37738, for current regulations on shelter use and camping.

Trail Location

The original route of the A.T. extended the entire length of the Great Smokies to Deals Gap. Beyond, the Trail traversed 3.3 mi. of privately owned land to Tapoco, where it crossed the Little Tennessee and Cheoah Rivers on a highway bridge and then led back east along the crest of the Yellow Creek Mtns. This route was necessitated because there was no other crossing of the Little Tennessee River.

The building of the TVA dam at Fontana on the Little Tennessee River made possible a relocation of the Trail that not only eliminated a difficult and circuitous route but added several unusual features to the Trail system:

Fontana Dam, which serves as a crossing of the Little Tennessee; a 29-mile-long lake that forms the southern boundary of the Great Smokies; and Fontana Village, which has become a recreational center. At the suggestion of the Smoky Mtns. Hiking Club, the Trail was relocated in 1946 and 1947 to leave the crest of the Smokies at Doe Knob, the point affording most direct access to Fontana Dam.

From here the route to Fontana Dam was constructed by NPS. Shuckstack, just off the route of the Trail, affords an outstanding grandstand view of the southern Appalachians. The relocation ascends from the dam to the original route on the crest of Yellow Creek Mtn. near High Top. The relocations shortened the original route by 11.7 miles.

This change in route eliminated from the Trail two outstanding features, Gregory Bald and Parson Bald. However, since the establishment of the Park and the suspension of grazing, these balds have tended to become overgrown and their open features, which constituted their outstanding attraction, are rapidly disappearing.

A portion of the original route has been officially designated as Gregory Bald Trail and continued as a side trail.

Geology

The following comment with respect to the geological structure of the Great Smoky Mtns., which is exposed at Newfound Gap, is quoted from *Nature Notes* (October 1939) by the Park Service:

"Great Smoky Mountains Expose Oldest Rock Strata in East

"Motorists in the Great Smoky Mountains National Park who travel over the new highway from Gatlinburg, Tennessee, to the Continental Divide, at Newfound Gap, and thence down to the village of Cherokee, North Carolina, may view one of the finest geological sections exposed in the entire East.

"Along this scenic drive, which mounts to over 5,000 feet above sea level, rock layers of slate, quartzite and conglomerate, tilted at astonishing angles, confirm the account given by geologists of how these very ancient mountains were brought forth. The Appalachians, which probably have been much higher in past aeons than now, have been elevated and worn down not once but several times. Originally some of the strata laid down in prehistoric seas as muds and sands contained fossil. These fossil-bearing rocks either have been worn away or so layered by heat and pressure that few evidences of the life that existed during their formation have been found up to the present time."

25

Fontana Dam and Fontana Village

Fontana Dam, part of the TVA system, was constructed on the Little Tennessee River during World War II to furnish hydroelectric power. The dam is 480 ft. high, the highest in the East and the sixth highest in the United States. The powerhouse and penstock are at the bottom near the center of the river channel. An inclined railway leads from the powerhouse to the visitors building at the top of the dam. TVA ceased operating the railway in October 1980, and at press time it was uncertain when operation might resume.

In May 1946 Fontana Village, which had been constructed at Welch Cove to house TVA construction works, was transferred to Government Services, Inc., for operation as a public recreation area. The village is some 3 mi. from the dam and at an elevation of 1,800 ft., immediately at the base of the Yellow Creek Mtns. Extensive facilities are available here, including a lodge, cafeteria, drug store, grocery store, post office, laundry, and medical center, and some 300 houses.

Government Services, Inc., has an extensive recreation program under the direction of a recreational supervisor. Hiking, fishing, horseback trips, and flower walks are particularly featured.

The area of Fontana Village is covered by the USGS Fontana Dam, N.C., quadrangle. Booklets on Fontana and a Fontana Village Location Map may be obtained by addressing Government Services, Inc., Fontana Dam, N.C. 28733.

The dam, in creating the lake with a normal shoreline at an elevation of about 1,710 ft., flooded out N.C. 288 from Deals Gap to Bryson City. A hard-surfaced road, N.C. 28, leads from U.S. 129 to Fontana Dam (9.5 mi. from Deals Gap) and continues to a junction with U.S. 19, 9 mi. south of Bryson City.

DAVENPORT GAP (TENNESSEE 32-NORTH CAROLINA 284) TO NEWFOUND GAP (TENNESSEE 71-U.S. 441)

Distance 30.8 miles

Brief Description of Section

This section traverses the wildest and once the most difficult portion of the Great Smokies. From Davenport Gap (1,975 ft.) there is a long, continuous climb of 3,025 ft. over a distance of 5.2 mi. to the crest of the state line, west of Mt. Cammerer, the eastern beginning of the Great Smokies.

Beyond there are many deep gaps and high peaks, with 11 major climbs and the same number of descents. After passing over Cosby Knob, the Trail swings around Mt. Guyot, a short distance from its 6,621-ft. summit. The next peaks are Tri-Corner Knob, Mt. Chapman, Mt. Sequoyah, Pecks Corner, Porters Mtn., and Charlies Bunion. After passing Mt. Kephart, the Trail descends 955 ft. to Newfound Gap.

The route through the section is graded, with a grade of no more than 15 percent. The Trail is maintained so that one can enjoy the continuous succession of panoramic views without constant attention to the footway.

The route is indicated by white paint blazes as well as by the dug footway. Board signs mark intersections with side trails.

Because much of the Trail is on or near the state line, the slopes have been designated in the Trail data as N.C. or Tenn.

Points of Interest

The vegetation along this section is mainly spruce and fir, reminiscent of the North woods and much of it virgin forest. Unlike the broader crest, south and west of Newfound Gap the crest is narrow, particularly in the section known as Sawteeth, where one may stand astride the state line. The outstanding peaks are Mt. Kephart, named for the distinguished authority and author of "Our Southern Highlanders"; the Jump-Off, affording a magnificent view north of the entire range as far as Mt. Guyot; Mt. Chapman, named in honor of Colonel David C. Chapman, who was instrumental in establishing the Park; and Mt. Guyot, named for Arnold

Guyot, whose explorations prior to the Civil War and manuscript map constitute invaluable source material for a study of the region.

The eastern beginning of the Great Smokies is the conspicuous Mt. Cammerer (formerly White Rock), renamed to commemorate the outstanding services to the Great Smoky Mtns. National Park by former NPS Director Arno B. Cammerer. The stone tower (5,025 ft.) on Mt. Cammerer affords a 360° panorama of the Smokies. This is one of the most spectacular views along the Trail. Between Mt. Cammerer and Mt. Guyot is a section known as Hell Ridge because of the devastation caused by forest fires on the N.C. side, and which was once famous for its difficult travel.

The highest point on this section of the Trail is about 6,360 ft. where it swings around the Tenn. side of Mt. Guyot, a short distance below the 6,621-ft. summit.

From Charlies Bunion are extraordinary views: to the west is the Jump-Off and Mt. Kephart, to the northwest is Mt. LeConte, to the north are gorges on headwaters of Porters Creek, slightly east of north is Greenbrier Pinnacle, and to the east is the jagged knifelike section of the state line known as the Sawteeth Range. This spectacular formation on a densely forested ridgecrest was said to have been occasioned by a fire on the N.C. slope, following lumbering operations, and the washing off thereafter of the vegetation by severe storms, resulting in the present-day denudation.

Road Approaches

From Davenport Gap north via Tenn. 32, it is 26.5 mi. to Newport, from which, via I-40 and U.S. 70, it is 45.4 mi. to Knoxville (71.9 mi. from Davenport Gap); and via Tenn. 32 and 73 it is 30.6 mi. to Gatlinburg. To south via N.C. 284 and 276 it is 29 mi. to Dellwood, N.C., and U.S. 19, which leads to Asheville, 60 mi. from Davenport Gap. A shorter route to Newport (19 mi.) and to Asheville (57 mi.) is to follow N.C. 284 to Mt. Sterling Village (Big Creek Ranger Station and primitive campground short distance upstream), turn left on gravel road beside Big Creek, and continue through Waterville and across Browns Bridge to I-40. N.C. 284, while narrow and steep, affords extraordinary views of the eastern end of the Great Smoky Mtns. National Park.

There is no public transportation in Davenport Gap. William Hochstetler, who lives on N.C. 284 about 5 mi. south of Davenport Gap, has assisted hikers with car shuttling and parking and is available at any time.

Write to Mr. William Hochstetler, Waterville Star Route, Newport, Tenn. 37821. The same service is also offered by Mrs. Nina Valentine, Laurel Springs Motel, Highway 73, Cosby, Tenn. 37722 (615-623-2681).

Because of vandalism it is not advisable to leave cars overnight near Davenport Gap. Park them instead at the Big Creek Ranger Station.

The south end of the section at Newfound Gap is reached from the highway that crosses the Great Smoky Mtns. at Newfound Gap. By this highway it is 16 mi. to Gatlinburg and 55 mi. to Knoxville, both in Tenn., and 20 mi. to Cherokee, N.C.

Maps

For detailed maps, see USGS Clingmans Dome, N.C.-Tenn., Mt. LeConte, Tenn.-N.C., Mt. Guyot, Tenn.-N.C., Luftee Knob, N.C.-Tenn., Hartford, Tenn.-N.C., and Waterville, Tenn.-N.C., quadrangles.

Shelters, Campsites, and Water

There are five shelters and 15 sources of water on the section. The shelters are listed below.

Miles from Davenport Gap	Shelter
0.9	Davenport Gap
7.9	Cosby Knob
15.6	Tri-Corner Knob
20.5	Pecks Corner (0.4 mi. from A.T.)
27.9	Ice Water Spring

Public Accommodations and Supplies

There are no public accommodations or supplies available on or near the Trail at either end of this section. Stores, post offices, restaurants, and lodging are available at Newport, Cosby, Gatlinburg, and Cherokee.

Precautions

The many deep gaps and high peaks along the Trail in this section involve considerably more climbing than a casual inspection of the route would indicate. Allowances of extra time and exertion should be made.

The section is easier to hike from southwest to northeast, from Newfound Gap (5,045 ft.) to Davenport Gap (1,975 ft.), than in the reverse direction. In traversing the section from southwest to northeast the climbing totals 4,608 ft. and the downhill travel 7,678 ft.

See information in the immediately preceding section (The Trail in the Great Smokies National Park) for advice about firewood, scarcity of water, wildlife protection, bears, and camping permits.

Trail Description, North to South

Miles	Data
0.0	From Davenport Gap at highway (Tenn. 32 and N.C. 284) follow graded trail W and cross small clearing.
0.2	*Water* can be found in field below and to left of Trail.
0.9	*Davenport Gap Shelter* is located 100 yd. to right of Trail, with *spring* nearby. Ascend steadily.
2.8	Reach lower Mt. Cammerer Trail from Cosby Campground on Tenn. side.
3.1	Reach side trail on left leading 50 yd. to *spring*.
3.2	Cross spur on N.C. side, ascend and skirt S slope of Mt. Cammerer (note spectacular trail construction).
4.4	Pass through gap in spur off side of Mt. Cammerer and ascend slope of mountain.
4.7	Reach small *campsite* (uphill) used by CCC in construction of Mt. Cammerer tower; just beyond is *spring* on right.
5.0	Reach graded side trail on right leading 0.6 mi. to Mt. Cammerer tower. Beyond side trail, route continues to ascend.
5.2	Cross high point (about 5,000 ft.); then cross spur on Tenn. side of Sunup Knob (5,050 ft.). There are good views.
6.5	Cross crest of Rocky Face Mtn., a spur on Tenn. side.
7.1	Descend to Low Gap (4,242 ft.). Trails lead from here to Walnut Bottom (N.C. side) following Low Gap Branch and to Cosby Campground (Tenn. side) following Cosby Creek 2.6 mi. From Low Gap climb 785 ft. to Cosby Knob.
7.8	*Water* crosses Trail.
7.9	Reach *Cosby Knob Shelter* 150 ft. to left, with *spring* nearby. Trail leaves virgin forest and enters a 4-mi. section known as Hell Ridge.
8.5	Cross spur on Tenn. side after swinging around N.C. side of Cosby Knob (5,145 ft.).
9.0	Cross spur and pass around forested side of Ross Knob (5,025 ft.) on Tenn. side.

9.4   Reach Camel Gap (4,645 ft.). Yellow Creek Trail leads to Big Creek and Walnut Bottom from here. Ascend, swinging to Tenn. side.

10.5   Reach wooded side of Camel Hump Knob (5,250 ft.).

11.7   Reach Maddron Bald Trail, which joins A.T. from Tenn. side. (This trail goes by Maddron Bald and Indian Camp Creek to Tenn. 73, with branch trail down Snake Den Mtn. to Cosby Campground. There is official primitive *campsite* with *spring* about 0.8 mi. down Maddron Bald Trail.) Follow A.T. around slope of Inadu Knob (5,941 ft.). (''Inadu'' means ''snake'' in Cherokee and refers to snake dens on mountainside.)

12.0   Reach Yellow Creek Gap.

12.6   Reach Deer Creek Gap (6,020 ft.). From here there are fantastic views of Mt. Guyot, Luftee Knob, Balsam Corner, and Mt. Sterling.

12.8   Leave burned-over section and enter virgin balsam fir and red spruce forest.

13.1   Here is good view of English Mtn. in Tenn. Trail ascends.

13.2   Cross Pinnacle Lead, spur off Tenn. side of Old Black.

13.4   Reach gap between Mt. Guyot and Old Black.

13.5   Reach faint trail, obstructed by blowdowns, leading up N slope of Mt. Guyot. (Climb requires about 1 hr. to reach top of second highest peak in Great Smokies.)

13.6   Pass *Guyot Spring*.

14.4   Cross Guyot Spur (6,360 ft.), which is highest point on A.T. in eastern part of Smokies. Trail descends, passing through most dense forest of balsam and spruce in Great Smokies.

15.0   Reach sharp-ridged gap between Tri-Corner Knob and Mt. Guyot; then climb along Tenn. side of Tri-Corner Knob (6,100 ft.). (Here begins N.C. side of Three Forks Wilderness Area. Balsam Mtn., leading from Tri-Corner Knob, forms boundary between Swain and Haywood Counties of N.C. Tri-Corner Knob is junction of two major ranges, the Smoky and the Balsam, and was given its name by geographer Arnold Guyot.)

15.4   Balsam Mtn. Trail, which leads to Hyatt Ridge and Round Bottom, comes in on left. (*Laurel Gap Shelter* is 6 mi. via this trail; accommodates 12; *spring* nearby.)

15.6   Come to trail junction. To follow A.T. bear right. Left fork leads 100 yd. to *Tri-Corner Knob Shelter* on N.C. side. (Built-in wire bunks accommodate 12; spring₁ nearby.)

15.7 Reach Big Cove Gap (5,825 ft.). Ascend, following state line between north and middle peaks of Mt. Chapman.

16.5 Reach high point of Trail on Mt. Chapman.

17.2 Reach Chapman Gap (5,650 ft.) and pass through beautiful virgin balsam and spruce forest.

17.8 Reach high point of Mt. Sequoyah (6,000 ft.).

18.5 Cross Old Troublesome, a spur off Tenn. side of Mt. Sequoyah. Trail leads through another magnificent forest of virgin conifers as it descends along Tenn. slope.

18.8 Reach Cooper Gap (5,650 ft.); then climb 250 ft. to Eagle Rocks.

19.5 Find *water* 800 ft. down N.C. side on N end of Eagle Rocks.

19.6 Reach spectacular view of precipitous slopes and sharp gorges caused by headwaters of Eagle Rocks Creek.

20.0 Swing around W peak of Eagle Rocks (5,900 ft.) and then around N.C. side of Pecks Corner, junction of Hughes Ridge and state line.

20.5 Reach Hughes Ridge Trail on left. (This is side trail to *Pecks Corner Shelter* (formerly Hughes Ridge). Built-in bunks accommodate 12 persons; *spring* nearby. To reach shelter follow graded Hughes Ridge Trail S for 0.4 mi. to gap and then turn left, downhill 100 yd. in beech woods.) N.C. side of Three Forks Wilderness Area ends here. About 100 ft. beyond junction of Hughes Ridge Trail is intermittent *spring* on right side of A.T.

20.7 Cross Hughes Ridge.

21.0 Cross unnamed ridge on N.C. side and then go through a typical virgin balsam and spruce forest. (There are good views of Laurel Top and Sawteeth Range, with Mt. LeConte visible through False Gap.)

21.8 Reach Bradleys View on state line, affording unusually fine views into deep-cut gorge of Bradley Fork and over mountains in N.C.

23.1 Cross Woolly Tops Lead. Three Forks Wilderness Area ends here.

23.4   Pass around side of Laurel Top (5,865 ft.).

24.4   Reach False Gap (5,400 ft.). (Site of the original Porters Gap has been subject of considerable controversy; the conflicting sites are Porters Gap and False Gap. Porters Gap, beyond on Trail, is at extremely high elevation, which worked against its final acceptance as the true gap. The name False Gap was applied to contrast to Porters Gap.) From False Gap, Trail gains 100 ft. in ascent of Porters Mtn., passing through dense forest of balsam and spruce.

25.0   Reach Porters Gap (5,500 ft.) on state line, very near junction of Porters Mtn. and state line ridge. Trail leads along crest of jagged range, known as the Sawteeth.

26.3   Come into 0.8 mi. section that was swept by fire following lumbering operations in 1925. (The tragic results are partly offset by spectacular views.)

26.4   Pass Richland Mtn. Trail, which comes in on left from Smokemont Campground, 8.5 mi. distant. (Via this trail and Grassy Branch Trail, it is 3.8 mi. to *Kephart Prong Shelter;* accommodates 12; provides *creek water*.)

26.5   Reach Dry Sluice Gap (5,375 ft.). (*Water* may be found about 400 ft. down N.C. side. Primitive trail leads down extremely steep Tenn. side to Porters Flats and Greenbrier.) Beyond, ascend along fire-scarred ridge.

26.7   Pass around higher peak of Charlies Bunion and then around right side of precipitous W (lower) peak of the Bunion. (Lower or W peak is sometimes called Fodder Stack; higher peak is called Charlies Bunion.)

27.0   Pass from the fire-scarred area into virgin forest.

27.8   Pass *spring* on right.

27.9   Reach *Ice Water Spring Shelter* on left. (Built-in wire bunks accommodate 12. *Water* is at spring on trail 0.1 mi. S.)

28.1   Boulevard Trail enters on right. (On Boulevard Trail it is 5.2 mi. to LeConte Lodge and Shelter. Accommodations are available at lodge from April 15 to late October. Shelter accommodates 12. About 100 yd. from A.T., spur trail off of Boulevard Trail leads 0.8 mi. to Mt. Kephart (6,150 ft.) and the Jump-Off (6,100 ft.). There are spectacular views from the Jump-Off.)

28.4	Reach elevation of about 6,000 ft. and begin gradual descent to Newfound Gap.
28.9	Here are fine views of Clingmans Dome (6,643 ft.), highest point in Park, to SW and of Thomas Ridge and Oconaluftee River gorge to S.
29.1	Reach, on state line, Sweat Heifer Trail, which leads down Kephart Prong on N.C. side. (The name Sweat Heifer is probably derived from old-time practice of driving cattle up this steep trail to high, grassy pastures. *Kephart Prong Shelter* is 3.5 mi. down this trail; accommodates 12; provides creek *water*.)
30.8	Reach crest of highway in Newfound Gap (5,045 ft.).

Trail Description, South to North

Miles   **Data**

0.0	From crest of highway at Newfound Gap (5,045 ft.), at NE corner of parking place, follow graded NPS Trail NE, along N.C. side through virgin forest of hardwoods and conifers. (The hardwoods are mainly yellow birch, while the conifers are red spruce and Fraser Fir, locally called balsam.) This section lies in Swain County, N.C.
0.5	Cross to Sevier County on Tenn. side. Follow state line.
1.6	Pass graded Sweat Heifer Trail leading down Kephart Prong. (The name Sweat Heifer is probably derived from old-time practice of driving cattle up this steep trail to high, grassy pastures. On N.C. side via this trail Kephart Prong Shelter is 3.5 mi.; accommodates 12; creek *water*.)
1.8	Here are fine views of Clingmans Dome (6,643 ft.), highest point in Park, to SW and of Thomas Ridge and Oconaluftee River gorge to S.
2.4	On state line, begin descent from elevation of about 6,000 ft.
2.6	At trail junction, take *right fork*. (Left is Boulevard Trail. On Boulevard Trail it is 5.2 mi. to *LeConte Lodge and Shelter.* Accommodations are available at lodge from April 15 to late October. Shelter accommodates 12. About 100 yd. from A.T., spur trail off of Boulevard Trail leads 0.8 mi. to Mt. Kephart (6,150 ft.) and the Jump-Off (6,100 ft.) There are spectacular

views from the Jump-Off.) From junction with Boulevard Trail, swing around N.C. side of Mt. Kephart.

2.9   Reach *Ice Water Spring Shelter*. (Built-in wire bunks accommodate 12 persons. *Spring* is 75 yd. farther on trail.) Beyond, descend.

3.8   Pass from virgin forest into 0.8-mi. section which was swept by fire after lumbering operations in 1925. (Tragic results of fire are partly offset by spectacular views.)

4.0   Pass around left side of precipitous W (lower) peak of Charlies Bunion.

4.1   Pass around higher peak of Charlies Bunion. (Lower (W) peak is sometimes called Fodder Stack and (E) higher peak Charlies Bunion.)

4.3   Descend to Dry Sluice Gap (5,375 ft.). (*Water* may be found about 400 ft. down N.C. side. Primitive side trail leads down extremely steep Tenn. side to Porters Flats and Greenbrier.)

4.4   Reach junction with Richland Mtn. Trail. Take left fork. (Right leads to Smokemont Campground; via this trail and Grassy Branch Trail, it is 3.8 mi. to *Kephart Prong Shelter*; accommodates 12; provides creek *water*.)

4.5   Pass out of fire scar and follow along sharp crest of Sawteeth Range.

5.4   Pass through Porters Gap (5,500 ft.) near junction of Porters Mtn. and state line ridge. (The site of original Porters Gap has been the subject of considerable controversy; conflicting sites are Porters Gap and False Gap. Porters Gap is an extremely high elevation, which worked against its final acceptance as the true gap.)

5.5   Cross crest of Porters Mtn. on Tenn. side.

6.1   Cross spur of ridge on Tenn. side and continue descent.

6.4   After drop of 100 ft. from Porters Mtn., reach False Gap (5,400 ft.). (The name False Gap was applied to contrast to Porters Gap.) Ascend steeply for 0.3 mi., and then more gradually.

7.4   Pass around side of Laurel Top (5,865 ft.).

7.6   Cross Woolly Tops Lead. (Here Three Forks Wilderness Area, established by NPS, begins on Tenn. side; on N.C. side Wilderness Area commences 7.5 mi. farther E at Hughes Ridge.

The Research Reservation is to be maintained as a wilderness area, with no development of any kind.) Descend again, after having gained some 400 ft. in elevation since leaving False Gap.

9.0　On state line is Bradleys View, affording unusually fine views into deepcut gorge of Bradley Fork and over mountains in N.C.

9.6　Commence ascent around Pecks Corner. (Here is junction of Hughes Ridge and state line range. Behind are good views of Laurel Top and the Sawteeth Range with Mt. LeConte visible through False Gap.)

9.8　Pass through typical virgin balsam and spruce forest and cross unnamed ridge on N.C. side.

10.0　Cross Hughes Ridge.

10.2　Keep straight ahead at junction with graded Hughes Ridge Trail. (This is side trail to *Pecks Corner Shelter*, formerly Hughes Ridge Shelter. Built-in wire bunks accommodate 12; *spring* nearby. To reach shelter, follow graded Hughes Ridge Trail S for 0.4 mi. to gap and then turn left, downhill 100 yd. in beech woods.) N.C. side of Three Forks Wilderness Area commences here. Beyond, Hughes Ridge Trail continues to Smokemont Campground.

10.3　Follow state line with good views of Eagle Rocks, Mt. Sequoyah, Chapman, and Guyot.

10.8　Swing to N.C. side around W peak of Eagle Rocks (5,900 ft.).

11.2　Reach spectacular view of precipitous Tenn. slope and into sharp gorges carved out by headwaters of Eagle Rocks Creek. (Trail has ascended 500 ft. from gap just W of Pecks Corner and Hughes Ridge.)

11.3　At N end of Eagle Rocks, *water* is found about 800 ft. down N.C. side.

11.9　Enter Copper Gap (5,650 ft.).

12.0　Swing to Tenn. side through magnificent stand of virgin conifers.

12.3　Cross Old Troublesome, a spur off Tenn. side of Mt. Sequoyah.

12.9　Cross high point of Mt. Sequoyah (6,000 ft.).

13.6　Reach Chapman Gap (5,650 ft.). From Chapman Gap, follow N.C. side and pass through virgin forest of balsam and spruce.

13.9	Cross spur on N.C. side.
14.3	Reach high point of Trail on Mt. Chapman, having climbed 600 ft. from Chapman Gap.
15.0	Reach Big Cove Gap (5,825 ft.). Ascend Tri-Corner Knob.
15.2	Come to trail junction. To follow A.T. bear left. Right leads 100 yd. to *Tri-Corner Knob Shelter* on N.C. side. (Built-in wire bunks accommodate 12; *spring* nearby.)
15.4	Reach junction with side trail. A.T. turns left. (Right is graded Balsam Mtn. Trail to Hyatt Ridge and Round Bottom on N.C. side. *Laurel Gap Shelter* is 6 mi. via this trail; accommodates 12; spring nearby.) Swing to Tenn. side and climb around side of 6,100 ft. Tri-Corner Knob. (Here N.C. side of Three Forks Wilderness Area ends. Tri-Corner Knob is at junction of two major ranges, the Smoky and the Balsam, and was given its name by geographer Arnold Guyot. Balsam Mtn., leading off from knob, forms boundary between Swain and Haywood Counties of N.C.)
15.7	Follow state line through sharp-ridged gap between Tri-Corner Knob and Mt. Guyot. (Here are fine views into N.C., particularly of Mt. Sterling and N.C. side of Hell Ridge.) Follow Tenn. slope of Mt. Guyot through what is probably densest stand of balsam and spruce in Great Smokies.
16.4	Cross Guyot Spur, leaving Three Forks Wilderness Area. (Elevation here is 6,360 ft., highest point on A.T. in eastern part of Great Smokies but 261 ft. below summit of Mt. Guyot; from last gap there has been net ascent of 290 ft.)
17.2	Reach *Guyot Spring.*
17.3	Faint, ungraded trail, badly obstructed by blowdowns, leads right, up N slope of Mt. Guyot (6,621 ft.). (Climb requires about 1 hr. to reach top of second highest peak in Great Smokies.) After dropping 130 ft. from Guyot Spur, reach gap between Guyot and Old Black.
17.6	Cross Pinnacle Lead, a spur off Tenn. side of Old Black. (Pinnacle Lead forms boundary between Sevier and Cocke Counties of Tenn. From here to Davenport Gap, in the main, Trail descends.) Note pleasing view of English Mtn. in Tenn. and of valley sections at foot of Great Smokies.
18.1	Leave virgin forest and enter Hell Ridge, so named because of

devastation resulting from forest fire on N.C. side along 4-mi. section of ridge, following lumbering operations.

18.2   Follow state line through Deer Creek Gap (6,020 ft.). Here are good views, particularly of Mt. Guyot, Luftee Knob, Balsam Corner, and Mt. Sterling, with their sharply defined ridges reaching down to Big Creek.

18.8   Reach Yellow Creek Gap. Swing around slope of Inadu Knob (5,941 ft.). ("Inadu" means "snake" in Cherokee and refers to snake dens on mountainside.)

19.1   Keep straight ahead at junction with Trail on Tenn. side. (Trail to left, Maddron Bald Trail, leads via Maddron Bald and Indian Camp Creek to Tenn. 73, with branch trail down Snake Den Mtn. to Cosby Campground. There is an officially designated and primitive *campsite,* with *spring,* about 0.8 mi. down Maddron Bald Trail; descent from A.T. to campsite is gradual.) Swing to Tenn. side around wooded side of Camel Hump Knob (5,250 ft.).

21.3   Reach Camel Gap (4,645 ft.). (Side trail on N.C. side, Yellow Creek Trail, leads down to Big Creek and Walnut Bottoms.) Pass around forested side of Ross Knob (5,025 ft.) on Tenn. side.

22.0   Forest growth on Tenn. side changes from coniferous to deciduous, largely oaks, beeches, maples, and a few chestnuts that have survived the blight.

22.3   Pass around N.C. side of Cosby Knob (5,145 ft.). Trail passes out of fire-denuded Hell Ridge and through virgin forests on both sides.

22.8   *Cosby Knob Shelter* is 150 ft. to right. (Built-in bunks accommodate 12; *spring* nearby.)

22.9   *Water* is 100 yd. below Trail.

23.0   *Water* crosses Trail.

23.6   Reach Low Gap (4,242 ft.), having descended 758 ft. from Cosby Knob. (From Low Gap, side trails lead down into both states; that on N.C. side, Walnut Bottoms Trail, follows Low Gap Branch, and then swings W near Walnut Bottoms; that on Tenn. side, Cosby Trail, follows Cosby Creek 2.6 mi. to Cosby Campground.)

24.2   Cross crest of Rocky Face Mtn., spur on Tenn. side. In 0.5

	mi., cross spur of Tenn. side of Sunup Knob (5,050 ft.). Beyond are many fine views in all directions.
25.6	After gaining 758 ft. in ascent from Low Gap, cross high point (about 5,000 ft.) and begin long descent toward Davenport Gap.
25.7	Where A.T. bears right, side trail continues ahead 0.6 mi. along state line to Mt. Cammerer (formerly White Rock) at E end of Great Smokies.
26.0	Pass *spring*. Just beyond, uphill, is small *campsite* used by CCC in constructing Mt. Cammerer tower.
26.3	Pass through gap in spur off N.C. side of Mt. Cammerer. (Here, descending along side of high rock cliff, is spectacular piece of trail construction.)
27.5	Cross spur on N.C. side.
27.7	Side trail leads right 50 yd. to *spring*.
27.9	Lower Mt. Cammerer Trail from Cosby Campground, 7.8 mi. distant, comes in on Tenn. side.
29.8	Pass trail leading 100 yd. left to *Davenport Gap Shelter*. (Built-in wire bunks accommodate 12; *spring* nearby.)
30.6	Cross small clearing. *Water* is in old field to right and below Trail.
30.8	Reach Davenport Gap (1,975 ft.) at NE end of Great Smoky Mtns. National Park.

Horsetails

NEWFOUND GAP (TENNESSEE 71-U.S. 441)
TO LITTLE TENNESSEE RIVER (FONTANA DAM)

Distance 37.8 miles

Brief Description of Section

From the north end of this section, at Newfound Gap, to Clingmans Dome (7.5 mi.), the Trail was constructed by the CCC in 1939-40. It is a graded foot trail, about 4 ft. wide. This portion of the Trail generally follows the state line on the crest of the ridges and lies entirely on the north side of the highway that was constructed from Newfound Gap to the Forney Ridge parking area on the south slope of Clingmans Dome. Rarely is the highway visible from the Trail. This link replaces the former route, which had become unsatisfactory after road construction.

From Clingmans Dome, the Trail follows the main crest of the Smokies to Silers Bald. West of Silers Bald, the Trail passes through several open gaps and bald knobs, the most prominent of which is Thunderhead.

From Silers Bald, for some 20 mi., the Trail is not graded. It was cleared as a fire trail by NPS in 1931 and now is recleared annually as part of the Park Service trail maintenance program. No work has been done on the footway, but use of the Trail, even over the balds, has worn a footway that indicates the route. In addition the route is marked with white paint blazes.

Since the route generally follows the state line as far as Doe Knob, the slopes are designated as N.C. and Tenn.

After 30.4 mi. of travel from Newfound Gap, the Trail leaves the crest of the Great Smokies and turns south along a spur ridge, crossing Shuckstack to reach the Little Tennessee River at Fontana Dam.

Points of Interest

This section traverses the western half of the Great Smoky Mtns. National Park and contains some of the finest peaks of the Great Smokies — the balds. Particularly impressive are Thunderhead and Spence Field. The views from the tower on Clingmans Dome, the highest peak in the Great Smokies (6,643 ft.), from the Balds, and from the firetower on

Shuckstack are outstanding. Clingmans Dome is the highest point on the entire A.T.

Beyond Clingmans Dome, the Trail passes through typical southern Appalachian hardwood forests in marked contrast to the coniferous forests of the eastern Great Smokies. Some of the Trail is along a grass-grown ridge dotted with mature timber, affording delightful travel.

Situated in the center of a bowl of high surrounding mountains, Shuckstack affords one of the most extraordinary outlooks in the southern Appalachians. The crest line of the Great Smokies from Thunderhead to Clingmans Dome is prominent. Hangover, southwest of the Great Smokies, is particularly impressive. To the south are the extensive high mountains of the Nantahala National Forest. Below is Fontana Lake.

Road Approaches

The north end of the section is at Newfound Gap on the Tenn.-N.C. state line. U.S. 441-Tenn. 71 crosses the gap 55 mi. south of Knoxville, Tenn., 16 mi. south of Gatlinburg, Tenn., and 20 mi. north of Cherokee, N.C. There is no scheduled bus service through Newfound Gap.

The south end of the section is at Fontana Dam on the Little Tennessee River, 3 mi. north of Fontana Village, N.C., on N.C. 28. The village is 39 mi. west of Bryson City, N.C., by U.S. 19 for 14 mi. and N.C. 28 for 25 mi. Fontana Village may also be reached by taking U.S. 129 south 37 mi. to Deals Gap on the Tenn.-N.C. state line and then N.C. 28 east for 9 mi. There is no bus service to Fontana Village. Hikers may arrange to ride with the mail carrier between Maryville and Fontana. Inquiry should be made by writing to Mr. Henry Marrow, 1225 Hutton Street, Maryville, Tenn. 37801.

Maps

For detailed maps, see USGS Clingmans Dome, N.C.-Tenn., Silers Bald, N.C.-Tenn., Thunderhead, N.C.-Tenn., Cades Cove, Tenn.-N.C., and Fontana Dam, N.C., quadrangles. The Fontana Dam quadrangle was prepared before the graded trail was constructed on Shuckstack Ridge and does not indicate the present route on the ridge.

Shelters, Campsites, and Water

There are eight shelters and 19 sources of water on the section. The shelters are listed below.

Miles From Newfound Gap	Shelter
4.4	Mt. Collins
10.3	Double Springs Gap
12.0	Silers Bald
17.4	Derrick Knob
23.4	Spence Field
25.8	Russell Field
28.1	Mollies Ridge
32.6	Birch Spring

On the TVA Fontana Dam reservation just south of the dam is a shelter (constructed 1980) that accommodates 20 and provides a picnic area and, at the visitor center, showers.

Public Accommodations and Supplies

There are no public accommodations available at Newfound Gap.

From the parking place at the crest of Newfound Gap it is 16 mi. to Gatlinburg, Tenn., where there are excellent motels, restaurants, and sources of supplies. Here also is the NPS headquarters.

Fontana Village (P.O. Fontana Dam, N.C.) is 3 mi. from south end of this section. Fontana Village is operated by Government Services, Inc.; stores, cafeteria, post office, and excellent accommodations are available here.

History

At Indian Gap, an old road built by Colonel William Thomas during Civil War with Indian labor crosses the Trail and the state line. Only trail-like vestiges remain. This is the original transmountain road. It was built not only for general war purposes but also for obtaining saltpeter from Alum Cave Bluff, in an unsuccessful attempt to supply Confederate armies then under siege in eastern Va.

The correct location of Mt. Collins was once a subject of some controversy. An early USGS map had placed Mt. Collins east of Indian Gap (present Mt. Kephart). Considering the peak between Indian Gap and Clingmans Dome as nameless, Asheville citizens sponsored a movement to name it Mt. Kephart in honor of Horace Kephart, noted authority on the southern Appalachians. A Guyot manuscript and map disclosed that this peak had been originally named Mt. Collins, and this name was restored. At the suggestion of the Tennessee Nomenclature Committee and by action of the U.S. Geographic Board, the name of Kephart was applied to the prominent peak 3 mi. east of Newfound Gap.

About 0.2 mi. west of the summit of Mt. Collins was the site of Meigs Post. This was the starting point of Return J. Meigs's survey in 1802, the exact location of which, whether at this point or at Miry Ridge, was an issue in litigation involving the ownership of extensive timber lands.

Clingmans Dome was formerly known as Smoky Dome. It was renamed for Thomas Lanier Clingman, U.S. senator, mining prospector, and Civil War general who explored these mountains during the 1850's and thereafter extolled their virtues.

The Bote Mtn. Trail is the old Anderson Rd., which takes its name from the founder and former president of Maryville College. Anderson promoted the construction of this road from Tuckaleechee Cove up Bote Mtn. to the state line. The word "Bote" is the designation of the ridge which the majority of the Cherokee Indian labor force building the road voted the route should follow. There being no "v" sound in their language, they indicated their choice by saying "bote."

Precautions

Although this section is only 37 mi. long, because of its many ascents and descents, most travelers should allow at least three days for its traverse. The route is easier to hike from north to south because of the large difference in elevation between the two ends of the section.

Across the balds, the route is unmistakable in clear weather; but when it is cloudy, foggy, or dark, it is necessary to watch paint blazes on rocks and mowed strips.

See information immediately preceding section 1 (The Trail in the Great Smoky Mountains National Park) for advice about firewood, scarcity of water, wildlife protection, bears, and camping permits.

Trail Description, North to South

Miles	Data
0.0	From junction of Newfound Gap Rd. and Trail from Davenport Gap, cross parking area to its W end and descend through opening in guard wall at NW side of parking area. Follow graded Trail, paralleling Park Service Skyway (road), which extends 7.6 mi. to Forney Ridge Parking Area on S slope of Clingmans Dome. Highway is to left; pass rock retaining wall on left.
0.5	Continue straight ahead, where abandoned Thomas Ridge Trail leads left through tunnel under Skyway. Ascend along Tenn. slope through beech and spruce forest.
0.9	At top of ridge, old trail (former A.T.) comes in on left. Beyond, ascend slope of Mt. Mingus with view of Mt. LeConte through balsam trees to right.
1.2	Reach crest of Mt. Mingus ridge; follow crest and bear left. (Here obscure trail to right leads to summit of Mt. Mingus, 5,802 ft.) From crest, descend N.C. slope through balsam with glimpse of road 100 ft. to left.
1.6	Turn sharp left, after bearing right across state line.
1.7	Reach Indian Gap and cross grassy open slope on Tenn. side. (Skyway, from Newfound Gap to parking place on slope of Clingmans Dome, is on crest to left; fine view from N.C. side. Old road crosses Trail here. On Tenn. side road is known as Road Prong Trail. It is 4 mi. down road to Newfound Gap Rd. at Chimneys parking area.) At Indian Gap, enter woods on W slope and ascend Tenn. side, following graded Trail.
1.8	Turn sharp left onto state line ridge.
1.9	Keep right; left is old trail along crest.
2.2	Reach *Little Indian Gap*. To right, graded trail leads downhill 500 ft. to *spring* at site of burned Little Indian Gap Shelter. Follow state line ridge for next 1.9 mi.
4.4	Take left fork. (Trail to right leads to Sugarland Mtn. *Mt. Collins Shelter* is 0.5 mi. down this trail. Built-in wire bunks accommodate 12; *spring* nearby.)
4.6	Reach summit of Mt. Collins (6,188 ft.). (Summit is overgrown; 100 ft. beyond is partial view over N.C. side.) Descend

gradually from Mt. Collins; then descend steeply with fine views S.

5.5   Reach Collins Gap (5,886 ft.). Here Trail on Tenn. slope skirts Skyway, which is on state line.

6.5   Reach site of Old Buzzards Roost Camp; *water* is 100 yd. to left. Reach summit of Mt. Love (6,446 ft.); then descend into gap (6,366 ft.) at E base of Clingmans Dome. Beyond, ascend steeply to summit.

7.5   Reach *Clingmans Dome* (6,643 ft.). *This is highest point on A.T.* Rare mountain cranberry is abundant here. (Side trail to left leads 50 yd. to observation tower providing a splendid panoramic view above balsam fir trees. From tower paved path leads downhill 0.5 mi. to Forney Ridge parking area at end of Skyway, 7.6 mi. from Newfound Gap.) Continue ahead; then descend slightly along narrow ridgecrest to gap at N base of Mt. Buckley, with fine view over East, or Main, Prong of Little River on Tenn. side; Mt. LeConte is most prominent peak visible here.

7.9   Reach wide trail on left. (This is Forney Ridge Trail, leading 2.5 mi. to Andrews Bald and 12.5 mi. to Fontana Lake; also leads to Forney Ridge parking area.)

8.0   Ascend to summit of Mt. Buckley (6,582 ft.). Descend steeply for 0.2 mi.; then follow along ridge at head of Steel Trap Creek on N.C. side (burned over in 1925).

8.4   Follow narrow ridgecrest.

8.7   Enter growth of balsam; descend gradually.

9.8   Pass on Tenn. side junction of Goshen Prong Trail (leads to Goshen Prong, Little River, and 10 mi. to Elkmont). Descend slightly.

10.3 Reach Double Springs Gap (5,507 ft.) and *Double Springs Gap Shelter* (built-in wire bunks for 12). This gap is named for two *springs,* one on each slope, 15 yd. from crest on N.C. slope and 35 yd. on Tenn. side. From gap, ascend through beech woods toward open knob E of Silers Bald. Beyond, character of vegetation changes: spruce and fir growth becomes less dense and is succeeded by hardwoods, mainly beech.

10.8 Cross Jenkins Knob. Ahead is magnificent view of Silers Bald with Welch Ridge and High Rocks to left, Miry Ridge to right and Thunderhead in background. Beyond this knob, few conifers are seen along Trail. Follow narrow semiopen crest, crossing "The Narrows," where Trail has a devious course along ridgecrest, dropping a short distance down on Tenn. side to avoid ledges. Ascend through dense beech growth.

11.5   Take less worn, right fork, up hill, along backbone of ridge. (Left is graded Welch Ridge Trail, which leads about 8 mi. to High Rocks and 15 mi. to Fontana Lake. Use care here.) Ascend on switchbacks through dense woods.

11.6   Reach open crest of Silers Bald (5,607 ft.) and panoramic view. (Silers Bald is named for Siler family, who pastured cattle on it in summer, driving them up Welch Ridge.) From crest, bear slightly left along open slope and then bear right, descending along path through narrow, open field.

12.0   At edge of woods, trail to right leads 100 yd. to *spring.* Just beyond trail to spring, pass on right *Silers Bald Shelter.* (Built-in wire bunks accommodate 12.) Beyond shelter, follow ridgecrest through beech woods.

14.3   Descend steeply to Buckeye Gap (4,817 ft.). Faint trails here are on both sides; *water* is 200 yd. down N.C. slope.

14.8   Reach graded Miry Ridge Trail on right, which leads 9.2 mi. to Elkmont, former summer resort. Here keep on left fork.

15.1   Cross Cold Spring Knob (5,240 ft.). (Miry Ridge leads off on Tenn. side from Cold Spring Knob.)

16.6   Skirt N.C. slope of Mt. Davis (formerly known as Greenbrier Knob). Descend.

17.1   Reach Sams Gap (4,840 ft.). (Here graded Greenbrier Ridge Trail comes in on right; it leads 8 mi. to public road on Middle Prong Little River above Tremont Ranger Station. There is good *spring* 100 yd. down, and to left of, Greenbrier Ridge Trail.)

17.3   Cross spur of knob; then enter open field at far corner of Tenn. side.

17.4   Pass, on right, *Derrick Knob Shelter.* (Built-in wire bunks accommodate 12; *spring* nearby. This shelter is located where herder's cabin used to stand in what was once open field.) *Water* is found 50 yd. to right on Tenn. slope.

	Cross overgrown field.
17.5	Enter woods at far corner of field. From Derrick Knob Shelter to Thunderhead, Trail is more strenuous.
17.7	Cross Chestnut Bald.
18.4	Reach Sugar Tree Gap (4,435 ft.). (Note sugar maples.)
19.2	Enter Starkey Gap (4,500 ft.). (Now wooded, it was formerly grassgrown.)
19.8	Bear left along N.C. slope of wooded Brier Knob (5,215 ft.) and descend.
20.2	Pass ledge affording view into N.C. Go into semiopen sag and then descend steeply along worn trail, skirting Tenn. slope of knob.
20.4	Go into Mineral Gap (5,030 ft.).
21.1	Enter Beechnut Gap. *Water* is 75 yd. down Tenn. slope.
21.6	Ascend through laurel and rhododendron toward E summit of Thunderhead. Reach summit of Thunderhead (5,527 ft.). (Triangulation marker is here.) Shortly after, come onto open ridge, descending gradually with woods on left. Follow open ridgecrest. (Trail leads for some 2 mi. along open grassgrown crest, interspersed with wooded sections. Route is unmistakable in clear weather, but it is necessary to watch paint blazes on rocks and mowed strip when vision is restricted by fog or darkness. Views from Thunderhead are outstanding.)
21.7	Pass, on right, abandoned Defeat Ridge Trail.
22.3	Cross Rocky Top (5,441 ft.), from which there are views of Fontana Lake. Descend between jutting boulders and bear right.
22.9	Reach peak and turn right down slope. Watch carefully for this turn, particularly in foggy or rainy weather. Continue along ridgecrest. Come into historic Spence Field, picturesque mountain top meadow, following ridgecrest.
23.1	In grassy sag, Jenkins Ridge Trail leads left 7.5 mi. to fireroad at Flint Spring Gap. Follow right fork from intersection.
23.4	Pass Bote Mtn. Trail on right. This trail is excellent connection between Cades Cove and A.T. At 0.1 mi. below A.T., beside Bote Mtn. Trail, is *spring*. From junction with Bote Mtn. Trail, bear left and ascend field. Here are splendid views. Spence Field is often considered as W end of Thunderhead.

Almost immediately pass Eagle Creek Trail, which leads left 9 mi. to Fontana Lake. *Spence Field Shelter* is 250 yd. down this trail on Spence Cabin Branch of Gunna Creek, tributary of Eagle Creek. (Built-in wire bunks accommodate 12; *spring* nearby.) Enter woods and follow wide trail through sparse timber toward Little Bald. (This section affords very pleasant travel.)

24.5   Reach Little Bald. Turn left through meadow (splendid views S), and after 70 yd. turn right. Continue across meadow and enter woods.

24.9   Come into grassy Maple Sugar Gap (4,630 ft.).

25.5   Enter open McCampbell Gap (4,328 ft.), and at edge of woods at far end of clearing, skirt N.C. side of wooded McCampbell Knob.

25.8   Reach E end of Russell Field. (Graded trail to right leads 5.5 mi. to Cades Cove Picnic Area.) *Russell Field Shelter* is located at trail intersection. (Built-in wire bunks accommodate 14; *spring* is 150 yd. down trail to Cades Cove.) Skirt N.C. side of Russell Field in woods to far end of field.

26.3   Enter Big Abrams Gap (4,080 ft.).

26.5   Reach top of knob; then descend steeply.

26.6   Enter Little Abrams Gap (4,120 ft.). Ascend to right on Tenn. side switching back to grass-grown Trail toward summit of Locust Knob.

27.5   Reach crest and continue along open, grassy ridge.

28.0   Cross Devils Tater Patch (4,775 ft.).

28.1   At Gant Lot, pass *Mollies Ridge Shelter* (built-in wire bunks accommodate 14; *spring* nearby). Trail descends steadily for next mile.

29.1   Reach Ekaneetlee Gap (3,842 ft.). (Through here, old Egwanulti Gap, passed early Cherokee route crossing mountains from valley towns to overhill towns. Primitive trail to right, Ekaneetlee Branch Trail, brushed out in 1970, leads to Cades Cove, 5.8 mi.) *Water* is found 100 yd. down Tenn. slope. From gap ascend toward Powell Knob on worn trail, bearing right.

29.8   Begin to skirt N.C. side of Powell Knob (4,439 ft.).

30.0   Reach Mud Gap (4,260 ft.). Within 50 yd. leave gap and ascend Doe Knob.

30.4 Reach summit of Doe Knob (4,520 ft.). Here major change in route begins. Trail leaves crest of Great Smokies and turns S along spur ridge, crossing Shuckstack Mtn. to reach Little Tennessee River at Fontana Dam. (Originial A.T. route continued W over Gregory and Parson Balds to Deals Gap, a distance of 9.5 mi. Part of it is designated as Gregory Bald Trail. Via this trail *Moores Spring Shelter* is 2.6 mi.; accommodates six; *spring* nearby.) At crest of Doe Knob turn sharp left, crossing flat summit.

30.5 Begin descent along spur ridge with deep ravine on left. Beyond are outstanding views of crest line of Smokies from Thunderhead to Clingmans Dome. Ahead, Greer Knob is prominent.

31.1 Begin skirting right (W) slope of Greer Knob.

31.7 Return to ridgecrest on S slope of Greer Knob and descend for 250 ft.

31.8 Reach gap where *water* is located 100 yd. down slope on right. From gap, follow narrow ridgecrest.

32.6 Reach Birch Spring Gap (3,834 ft.). *Birch Spring Shelter* is 100 yd. to right down slope. (Built-in wire bunks accommodate 12; *spring* nearby.) Ahead is view of Shuckstack Mtn. firetower. From gap ascend steeply for 400 ft.; then follow ridgecrest and descend.

32.9 Reach Red Ridge Gap.

33.5 Reach Sassafras Gap (3,653 ft.). (To right, jeep road leads to fireroad at Twenty-mile Creek and to N.C. 28 at point 3.7 mi. from Deals Gap on U.S. 129.) From Shuckstack to Little Tennnessee River, terrain appears on USGS Fontana Dam quadrangle. This sheet, however, was prepared prior to construction of graded trail up Shuckstack Ridge and therefore does not show present route of A.T. along ridge. From Sassafras Gap, follow jeep road S toward prominent firetower on Shuckstack Mtn. (4,020 ft.).

33.8 Come onto ridgecrest in bend of road. (To left, road leads 0.1 mi. to firewarden's cabin and firetower on crest of Shuckstack. Firetower, by virtue of location on high side spur, presents one of the most extraordinary panoramic views of southern Appalachians. Crest line of Great Smokies from Thunderhead to Clingmans Dome is prominent. Hangover to SE and mountains to S in Nantahala National Forest are particularly imposing. Tower overlooks Fontana Lake. This view is feature of relocated trail.) Continue straight ahead, descending, on trail constructed by NPS in 1963.

34.0   Turn sharp left and see fantastic views to S.

34.6   Reach gap between Shuckstack and Little Shuckstack. Skirt around W side of Little Shuckstack.

34.9   At bend in Trail, variable *water* is few yards to left.

35.0   Reach ridgecrest and turn right, descending gradually.

36.9   Variable *spring* is 10 yd. to right.

37.2   Reach hard-surfaced road. Turn right along road and almost immediately reach intersection with dirt road (abandoned N.C. 288). Continue through intersection and follow hard-surfaced road along lakeshore for 0.6 mi. to N end of Fontana Dam. (From N end of dam hard-surfaced road leads downstream 0.2 mi. to parking overlook, which affords spectacular view of dam and powerhouse.) Continue past visitor center (showers and toilets) to reach Fontana Dam Shelter.

Rhododendron

Trail Description, South to North

Miles	Data
0.0	From end of Fontana Dam on N bank of Little Tennessee River follow hard-surfaced road to right along lakeshore for 0.6 mi. (From N end of dam hard-surfaced road leads downstream 0.2 mi. to parking overlook, which affords spectacular view of dam and powerhouse.)
0.6	Reach intersection with dirt road (abandoned N.C. 288). On far side of intersection turn left off hard-surfaced road and enter woods. Graded trail, constructed by NPS in 1963, ascends Shuckstack Ridge gradually, crossing old A.T. several times.
0.9	Variable *spring* is 10 yd. to left. Ascend.
2.7	Shuckstack firetower is visible ahead.
2.8	Begin skirting W side of Little Shuckstack.
2.9	In bend of Trail variable *water* is few yd. to right.
3.3	Reach gap between Little Shuckstack and Shuckstack.
3.6	Here is excellent view to S.
3.8	Turn sharp right, ascending.
4.0	Reach jeep road on ridgecrest. (To right, road leads 0.1 mi. to NPS cabin and firetower on Shuckstack (4,020 ft.).) A.T. continues straight ahead, descending on road.
4.3	Reach Sassafras Gap (3,653 ft.). To left jeep road leads to N.C. 28 at a point 3.7 mi. from Deals Gap on U.S. 129. From the gap follow jeep road ahead.
4.6	Come onto crest and ascend; then descend for 0.2 mi.
4.9	Reach Red Ridge Gap, ascend, and follow ridgecrest.
5.2	Descend steeply for 400 ft.
5.3	Reach Birch Spring Gap (3,834 ft.). To left 100 yd. down slope on worn trail is *Birch Spring Shelter*. (Built-in wire bunks accommodate 12; *spring* nearby.)
6.0	Reach gap at S base of Greer Knob. (*Spring* is 100 yd. to left down slope.) From gap, ascend for 250 ft. along crest.
6.1	Skirt W slope of Greer Knob for next 0.6 mi.
7.2	Reach sag at base of main crest of Great Smokies and ascend steeply.
7.3	Reach crest of ridge. Turn sharp right and reach Doe Knob in 400 ft. On Doe Knob (4,520 ft.), crest of Great Smokies is reached. (Here route turns right (E) and follows ridgecrest for

30.2 mi. farther to Newfound Gap. On left Gregory Bald Trail comes in (2.8 mi. to Gregory Bald).) From Doe Knob follow along level crest for 0.1 mi.; then descend.

7.8   Reach Mud Gap; then skirt N.C. side of Powell Knob (4,439 ft.).

8.0   Descend gradually for 0.7 mi.

8.7   Reach Ekaneetlee Gap (3,842 ft.). (Through here, old Egwanulti Gap, passed early Cherokee route crossing mountains from valley towns to overhill towns. Primitive trail to left, brushed out in 1970, leads 5.8 mi. to Cades Cove. *Water* is found 100 yd. down Tenn. slope.) Ascend steeply from Ekaneetlee Gap for 0.3 mi. on narrow trail. Beyond, ascend gradually along open ridge through sparse timber on wide trail.

9.7   Reach *Mollies Ridge Shelter*. (Built-in wire bunks accommodate 14; *spring* nearby.)

9.9   Cross Devils Tater Patch (4,775 ft.) and follow open, grassy ridgecrest.

10.3   Cross Locust Knob.

11.2   Reach Little Abrams Gap (4,120 ft.) and ascend steeply.

11.5   Reach Big Abrams Gap (4,080 ft.) and ascend steadily.

11.8   Skirt N.C. side of Russell Field in woods below edge of field.

12.0   At far end of Russell Field, bear right. (Graded trail to left leads 5.5 mi. to Cades Cove Picnic Area. *Russell Field Shelter* is at trail intersection. Built-in wire bunks accommodate 14. *Spring* is about 150 yd. down trail to Cades Cove.)

12.3   Reach grassy McCampbell Gap (4,328 ft.).

12.9   Enter grassy Maple Sugar Gap.

13.3   Reach edge of meadow (Little Bald) with excellent views to S, turn left for 70 yd., and leave meadow. Turn right and enter woods. Follow along flat crest through open parklike woods, descending slightly, and enter grassy Spence Field. There are splendid views here. (This is often considered W end of Thunderhead.)

14.4   Keep left, where Eagle Creek Trail on right leads 9 mi. to Fontana Lake. *Spence Field Shelter* is 250 yd. down this trail on Spence Cabin Branch of Gunna Creek, tributary of Eagle Creek. (Built-in wire bunks accommodate 12; *spring* nearby.)

4.5   Pass, on left, graded Bote Mtn. Trail. (Leads to Cades Cove, 5 mi.; Laurel Creek Road is 6.6 mi. This forms excellent connection between Cades Cove and A.T. At a distance of 0.2 mi. below A.T., beside Bote Mtn. Trail, is *spring*.) Keep slightly to right in open Spence Field. Here are splendid views. Descend steeply.

4.7   Enter grassy sag. Here Jenkins Ridge Trail to right leads 7.5 mi. to fire-road at Flint Spring Gap. From Spence Field, Trail leads for some 2 mi. along Thunderhead, open grass-grown crest, interspersed with wooded sections. (Route is unmistakable in clear weather, but it is necessary to watch paint blazes on rocks and mowed strips when vision is restricted by fog or darkness.) From sag ascend grassy and overgrown slope.

15.0   Reach W peak of Thunderhead (5,281 ft.) and turn sharp left. Descend steeply.

15.5   Reach summit of Rocky Top (5,441 ft.) and ascend between jutting boulders (notice view of Fontana Lake).

16.1   Pass abandoned Defeat Ridge Trail on left. From sag ascend gradually through heavy rhododendron growth, with woods on right.

16.2   Reach rhododendron-clad summit of Thunderhead (5,527 ft.). Triangulation marker is here.

16.7   Reach Beechnut Gap. (*Water* is 75 yd. down Tenn. slope.)

17.4   Reach Mineral Gap (5,030 ft.).

17.7   Pass through semi-open sag; pass ledge with fine views into N.C. side.

18.1   Swing around N.C. slope of wooded Brier Knob (5,215 ft.) (There is no trail to summit.) Return to crest and descend very steeply.

18.6   Reach Starkey Gap (4,500 ft.), formerly grass-grown, now wooded. Climb gradually along N.C. slope.

19.3   Enter Sugar Tree Gap (4,435 ft.). (Note sugar maples here. Faint trail on right leads down N.C. side.) Ascend along crest.

20.0   Pass through slight gap with good views of N.C.

20.2   Cross Chestnut Bald, with views on N.C. slope.

20.3   Enter overgrown field.

20.4   Reach *Derrick Knob Shelter* on left. (Built-in wire bunks accommodate 12; *spring* nearby. Shelter is located where herder's cabin used to stand, in what was once an open field. Keep left here. Beyond shelter, enter woods.

20.7   Enter Sams Gap (4,840 ft.). Here take right fork. (Left is graded Greenbrier Ridge Trail; leads 8 mi. down to public road on Middle Prong Little River above Tremont Ranger Station. There is good *spring* 100 yd. down and to left of Greenbrier Ridge Trail.) Continue along crest.

21.2   Swing around N.C. side of Mt. Davis (formerly Greenbrier Knob).

22.7   Reach Cold Spring Knob (5,240 ft.).

23.0   Pass Miry Ridge Trail on left, which leads 9.2 mi. to Elkmont, former summer resort.

23.2   Reach Buckeye Gap (4,817 ft.). (Faint trail here on both sides; *water* may be found about 200 yd. on N.C. slope.) Follow crest, alternately climbing and descending gradually through beech woods.

25.9   Reach *Silers Bald Shelter*. (Built-in wire bunks accommodate 12.) Just beyond shelter, trail to left leads 100 yd. to *spring*. Beyond side trail to spring, bear left.

26.0   Cross crest of Silers Bald (5,607 ft.). (Silers Bald is named for family who pastured cattle on it in summer, driving them up Welch Ridge. Here is good view of Mt. LeConte on Tenn. side. To S is Welch Ridge with firetower on High Rocks, near Park boundary; to E is good view of Clingmans Dome; high mountains are visible in all directions.) Descend on switchbacks to E.

26.1   Enter beech woods.

26.2   Pass Welch Ridge Trail on N.C. side (leads about 8 mi. to High Rocks and 15 mi. to Fontana Lake). Continue on well-worn trail, passing through two small grassy meadows from which good views of Silers Bald and other mountains are obtained.

27.0   Reach Jenkins Knob. (Use care here. Keep well to left, entering woods about 100 ft. before reaching summit of Jenkins Knob.) Descend gradually.

27.5   Reach Double Springs Gap (5,507 ft.) and *Double Springs Gap Shelter* (built-in wire bunks for 12). Name of gap indicates existence of two variable *springs*, one on each side of state line. Better spring is on N.C. side, only 15 yd. from actual crest; that on Tenn. side is 35 yd. from crest. Both springs flow into Tenn. River. From Double Springs Gap, ascend slightly.

28.0   Pass junction of Goshen Prong Trail on left (Tenn.) side (leads to Goshen Prong of Little River and Elkmont). Forest becomes largely spruce and balsam.

29.6   Climb through burned N.C. side of slope at head of Steel Trap Creek, re-entering virgin forest.

29.8   Cross summit of Mt. Buckley (6,582 ft.). Reach gap at N base of Mt. Buckley, with fine view over East, or Main, Prong of Little River on Tenn. side; Mt. LeConte is very prominent here.

29.9   Pass wide trail on right. (This is Forney Ridge Trail, leading 2.5 mi. to Andrews Bald and 12.5 mi. to Fontana Lake; it is also shortcut to Forney Ridge parking area.) Continue along crest.

30.3   Reach *Clingmans Dome* (6,643 ft.). *This is highest point on A.T.* Rare mountain cranberry is abundant here. (Side trail to right leads 50 yd. to observation tower, providing splendid panoramic view above balsam fir trees. From tower hard-surfaced path leads downhill 0.5 mi. to Forney Ridge parking area at end of Skyway, 7.6 mi. from Newfound Gap.) From Clingmans Dome descend steeply into gap. Beyond, ascend. Reach summit of Mt. Love (6,446 ft.); then descend gradually.

31.3   At site of Old Buzzards Roost Camp, *water* is 100 yd. to right. Descend steeply.

32.1   Skirt Skyway, which is on state line.

32.3   Reach Collins Gap. Beyond, ascend steeply; here are fine views.

33.2   Reach summit of Mt. Collins (6,188 ft.). (Summit overgrown; 100 ft. before reaching summit is partial view over N.C. side.) From summit of Mt. Collins, descend.

33.5   Trail from Sugarland Mtn. comes in on left. *Mt. Collins Shelter* is 0.5 mi. down this trail. (Built-in wire bunks accommodate 12; *spring* nearby.)

33.8   Trail to right leads 35 yd. to Skyway. Descend along Tenn. side.

34.5   Skyway is 100 ft. to right. Ascend and descend along State

Line Ridge.

35.3   Reach Little Indian Gap. (To left, graded trail leads downhill 500 ft. to *spring* at site of burned Little Indian Gap Shelter.) From Little Indian Gap ascend; old trail comes in on left on ridgecrest.

36.1   Reach Indian Gap at 35.9 mi. (Old road crosses state line here. On Tenn. side old road is known as Road Prong Trail; it leads 4 mi. to Chimneys parking area on Newfound Gap Rd.)

36.5   Bear right. Old obscure trail leading to summit of Mt. Mingus (5,802 ft.) leads to left.

36.6   Reach crest of Mt. Mingus Ridge. Beyond, descend slope, with views of Mt. LeConte through balsam trees to left. Descend along Tenn. slope through beech and spruce forest.

37.3   Continue ahead where abandoned Thomas Ridge Trail to right leads through tunnel under Skyway. Continue on Trail, paralleling Skyway and rock retaining wall on right.

37.8   Reach parking area at crest of ridge in Newfound Gap. Cross parking area to Trail on opposite (E) side. (Here is magnificent panoramic view. Particularly noteworthy is the Balsam range, "master" crosschain of Great Smokies.)

Trillium

SIDE TRAILS OF GREAT SMOKY MOUNTAINS
NATIONAL PARK

"Side trails" in this chapter include all the trails which branch directly from the A.T. and most of those which diverge from these side trails. Thus the chapter covers a large part, but not all, of the 800-mi. network of trails in the Great Smoky Mtns. National Park. Detailed descriptions of more than 500 trails in the Park are given in the *Hiker's Guide to the Smokies* by Dick Murlless and Constance Stallings (Sierra Club 1973).

Most of the side trails are standard 4-ft. graded paths; a few are narrower graded foot trails; and others are substandard or "primitive" trails. The last may be good or quite rough in places; they are sometimes overgrown in summer. When classified as a "manway," a trail is marked, but improved by only occasional cutting of limbs and brush sufficient to allow passage of hikers with packs.

With the discontinuance of the CCC, much of the Trail maintenance in the Smokies, because of inadequate appropriations and consequent lack of personnel, was necessarily curtailed. Even some of the less-used "grade A" trails may be overgrown in summer.

The listing of the side trails in this chapter begins at the northeast end of the Park at Davenport Gap and proceeds southwest to Fontana Dam.

Trails that originate at the A.T. are numbered and are referred to as leading north (into Tenn.) or south (into N.C.), although they do not necessarily follow the compass directions. Where such trails do not originate at a point named in the guide, a distance is given from the nearest named point. The diverging trails are lettered as subdivisions of the side trails from which they branch off; their beginnings are marked by distances from the A.T.

1. LOWER MT. CAMMERER TRAIL. Leaves A.T. 2.8 mi. W of Davenport Gap; leads N 7.8 mi. to public road at Cosby Campground on easy grade, going around N side of Mt. Cammerer (formerly White Rock), through young forest growth.

2. MT. CAMMERER TRAIL. Leaves A.T. 5.0 mi. W of Davenport Gap; leads NE 0.6 mi. along crest to Mt. Cammerer firetower. Passes through rhododendron, laurel, azalea, and over bare rock. Balcony of firetower is open, for view of entire horizon.

3. COSBY TRAIL. Leaves A.T. at Low Gap; leads N 2.6 mi. to public road at Cosby Campground. Passes through beech, birch, pine, and toward lower end, some large virgin hemlock. Lower end is on fire-road.

4. WALNUT BOTTOMS TRAIL. Leaves A.T. at Low Gap; leads S 59.5 mi. to Mt. Sterling Village. Passes through second-growth hardwoods along Low Gap Branch to Big Creek, up Big Creek, which is crossed at Walnut Bottoms, thence down Big Creek to Big Creek Primitive Campground near village of Mt. Sterling. Section from Walnut Bottoms to campground is on fire-road.

5. YELLOW CREEK TRAIL. Leaves A.T. at Camel Gap; leads 10.5 mi. to Big Creek Primitive Campground near Mt. Sterling Village. First 3 mi. is on burned-over mountainside, from which there are good views of Big Creek watershed. Next 1.5 mi. is along beautiful Mt. Guyot Creek. Remainder is on fire-road passing through Walnut Bottoms.

6. MADDRON BALD TRAIL. Leaves A.T. 2.2 mi. W of Camel Gap on E slope of Inadu Knob; leads N 7.2 mi. to Tenn. 73 at Valentine's nursery. First mile is through spruce-type forest and then over Maddron Bald, laurel slick, and down through virgin hardwoods and old fields. Lower end is on fire-road. There are large grapevines.
   6-A. SNAKE DEN MTN. TRAIL. Leaves No. 6 at 0.8 mi. N of A.T.; leads straight ahead 5.8 mi. to public road at Cosby Campground. Goes through pine and cove hardwood-type forest.

7. BALSAM MTN. TRAIL. Leaves A.T. at Tri-Corner Knob; leads S 9.5 mi. to Pin Oak Gap, where it intersects Heintooga-Round Bottom Rd. (open to one-way motor travel from Heintooga to Round Bottom, May through October; left on this road Balsam Mtn. Campground is 8.5 mi.; to right, public road at Round Bottom on Straight Fork is 5 mi.). Laurel Gap Shelter is 6 mi. from A.T. via this trail (accommodates 12; spring nearby).
   7-A. HYATT RIDGE TRAIL. Leaves No. 7 at 0.5 mi. S of A.T.; leads right to 8.8 mi. via Hyatt Ridge and Hyatt Prong to public

road on Straight Fork. This trail borders whole E side of Three Forks Wilderness Area. There are several very large black cherry trees.

7-B. BREAKNECK RIDGE TRAIL. Leaves No. 7-A at 5.2 mi. from No. 7; leads right 2 mi. to head of Raven Fork at "Three Forks" in heart of Three Forks Wilderness Area. Natural swimming pool is there. Trail is classified as "manway."

7-C. ROUND BOTTOM TRAIL. Leaves No. 7-A at 5.8 mi. from No. 7 (0.5 mi. W of Hyatt Bald); leads left 2.8 mi. to public road at Round Bottom on Straight Fork.

7-D. WILDERNESS TRAIL. Leaves No. 7-A at 6.8 mi. from No. 7; leads right 1 mi. to Raven Fork in Three Forks Wilderness Area.

7-E. GUNTER FORK TRAIL. Leaves No. 7 at 4.8 mi. S of A.T.; leads left 5 mi. to Walnut Bottoms. Trail is classified as "manway."

7-F. MT. STERLING GAP TRAIL. Leaves No. 7 at 5.8 mi. S of A.T.; leads left 7.5 mi. to N.C. 284 at Mt. Sterling Gap.

7-G. SWALLOW FORK TRAIL. Leaves No. 7-F at Pretty Hollow Gap, 4 mi. from No. 7; leads left 5 mi. to Walnut Bottoms.

7-H. PRETTY HOLLOW GAP TRAIL. Leaves No. 7-F at Pretty Hollow Gap, 4 mi. from No. 7; leads right at 5.2 mi. to public road in Cataloochee Cove.

7-I. MT. STERLING TRAIL. Leaves No. 7-F at 5 mi. from No. 7; leads left 0.5 mi. to Mt. Sterling firetower, with comprehensive view.

7-J. CRAIG BRANCH TRAIL. Leaves No. 7 at Mt. Sterling firetower; leads 5 mi. to Big Creek Primitive Campground, 1 mi. SW of village of Mt. Sterling. Trail is classified as "manway."

7-K. BAXTER CREEK TRAIL. Leaves No. 7-J at 1 mi. NE of Mt. Sterling firetower; leads 5.2 mi. to Big Creek Primitive Campground, 1 mi. SW of village of Mt. Sterling.

7-L. BEECH GAP TRAIL. Leaves No. 7 at 8 mi. S of A.T.; leads right 3 mi. to public road at Round Bottom on Straight Fork.

8. HUGHES RIDGE TRAIL. Leaves A.T. at Pecks Corner; leads S 10 mi. to public road at Smokemont Campground. Route is mostly through northern hardwoods, with exceptionally fine views of Three

Forks Wilderness Area and Bradley Fork virgin hardwood forest. At 5 mi. there is fine stand of flame azalea.

8-A. UPPER CREEK TRAIL. Leaves No. 8 at 2 mi. S of A.T.; leads right 7.5 mi. via Taywa Creek and Bradley Fork to public jeep road at Smokemont.

8-B. ENLOE CREEK TRAIL. Leaves No. 8 at 4.5 mi. S of A.T.; leads left 3 mi. to Raven Fork in Three Forks Wilderness Area.

8-C. CHASTEEN TRAIL. Leaves No. 8 at 5 mi. S of A.T.; leads right 5.5 mi. via Chasteen Creek to public road at Smokemont.

8-D. TOW STRING TRAIL. Leaves No. 8 at 8 mi. S of A.T.; leads left 6.5 mi. to public road below Smokemont. Trail is not maintained.

9. RICHLAND MTN. TRAIL. Leaves A.T. at Dry Sluice Gap; leads S 8.5 mi. to Smokemont via Tennessee Branch and Bradley Fork.

9-A. GRASSY BRANCH TRAIL. Leaves No. 9 at 1.8 mi. S of A.T.; leads right 4.5 mi. to Newfound Gap Rd. via Grassy Branch and Kephart Prong. Kephart Prong Shelter is 3.8 mi. from A.T. via this trail (accommodates 12; creek water).

10. BOULEVARD TRAIL. Leaves A.T. at crest of A.T. on shoulder of Mt. Kephart; leads N 5 mi. to Mt. LeConte. This is ridgecrest trail through spruce and fir with exceptional views of Porters Creek watershed. Views from peaks of Mt. LeConte are all-inclusive. From points near LeConte's High Top, trails lead left from Boulevard Trail to Myrtle Point and to Cliff Top, with spectacular views. Many of LeConte's ledges are covered with dwarf rhododendron and sand myrtle. There is a lodge on Mt. LeConte, open from April 15 to late October, where excellent accommodations are available. (Write LeConte Lodge, Gatlinburg, Tenn. 37738, for rates, closing date, and other information; lodge sometimes closes early because of weather conditions.) There is also a shelter beside Boulevard Trail near LeConte's High Top. (Built-in wire bunks accommodate 12. Spring is down Trillium Gap Trail below LeConte Lodge; see below.)

10-A. JUMP-OFF TRAIL. Leaves No. 10 at 0.1 mi. N of A.T.; leads right 0.8 mi. to the Jump-Off, rock ledge offering spectacular view into valleys of Porters Creek watershed, almost 1,000 ft.

below. Route also crosses summit of Mt. Kephart (6,200 ft.). To reach the Jump-Off, turn left at summit marker on Mt. Kephart and follow worn footway.

10-B. TRILLIUM GAP TRAIL. Leaves Mt. LeConte; leads 6.5 mi. to Roaring Fork Motor-Nature trail (open to one-way motor traffic from Cherokee Orchard down Roaring Fork, May through October). At 3.5 mi. (Trillium Gap), turn left.

10-C. TRILLIUM BRANCH TRAIL. Leaves No. 10-B at 3.5 mi. from Mt. LeConte at Trillium Gap; leads right 4.2 mi. to public road in Greenbrier Cove. At 2 mi. famous ''Fittified Spring'' is on right. Lower 1.2 mi. is on fire-road.

10-D. BRUSHY MTN. TRAIL. Leaves No. 10-B at Trillium Gap, 3.5 mi. from Mt. LeConte; leads straight ahead 0.3 mi. to summit of Brushy Mtn. This is not a standard trail.

10-E. RAINBOW FALLS TRAIL. Leaves Mt. LeConte; leads 6.8 mi. to public road at Cherokee Orchard. First section is down Rocky Spur, affording excellent views of valleys and farming country to the N. Passes Rainbow Falls.

10-F. BULL HEAD TRAIL. Leaves Mt. LeConte; leads 7.2 mi. to public road at Cherokee Orchard. Displays views of Sugarland Valley on West Prong of Little Pigeon River.

10-G. ALUM CAVE BLUFF TRAIL. Leaves Mt. LeConte; leads 5.2 mi. to Grassy Patch on Newfound Gap highway from Gatlinburg. Near start of trail, evidence of cloudburst that occurred in September 1951 may still be seen. At 3 mi. trail passes under Alum Cave Bluff and at 4.2 mi. through Arch Rock. From just below Bluff ''needle's eye'' is to be seen in ridge off to right.

11. SWEAT HEIFER TRAIL. Leaves A.T. 1 mi. W of crest of A.T on shoulder of Mt. Kephart; leads S 5.5 mi. to Newfound Gap road via Sweat Heifer Creek and Kephart Prong. Extends through severely burned-over area, now growing up in fire cherry and northern hardwoods. Presents good views of Oconaluftee Valley. Kephart Prong Shelter is beside this trail 3.5 mi. from A.T. (Built-in wire bunks accommodate 12 persons; creek water.)

12. ROAD PRONG TRAIL. Leaves A.T. at Indian Gap; leads N 4 mi. to

Newfound Gap Rd. at Chimneys parking area. A historic trail, it is original transmountain road, constructed by Colonel Thomas with Cherokee Indians during Civil War, not only for general war purposes but also for obtaining saltpeter from Alum Cave Bluff, in an unsuccessful attempt to supply Confederate armies then under seige in E Va. Has abundance of rhododendron among virgin hemlock and hardwoods. Except for last mile, this is not a standard trail. Crosses Road Prong several times.

12-A. CHIMNEYS TRAIL (replaces former steep route). Leaves No. 12 at 3 mi. N of Trail; leads left about 1.2 mi. to top of Chimneys.

13. FORK RIDGE TRAIL. Leaves A.T. at gap 0.5 mi. E of Mt. Collins; leads S 16.5 mi. to public road at Deep Creek Ranger Station via Fork Ridge and Deep Creek to Bryson Place (6.2 mi. from A.T.) and Sunkota Ridge. First mile is through virgin spruce and fir; to Deep Creek Gap, through northern hardwoods; and to Bryson Place, through virgin hardwoods.

14. SUGARLAND MTN. TRAIL. Leave A.T. 0.2 mi. E of Mt. Collins; leads N 12 mi. to Little River Rd. at Fighting Creek Gap. Offers excellent views of Mt. LeConte and Sugarland and Little River valleys.

14-A. ROUGH CREEK TRAIL. Leaves No. 14 about 4.5 mi. from A.T.; leads left 6.4 mi. to public road 1 mi. S of Elkmont. Lower 3 mi. is on fire-road, which is open to motor travel May through October. Trail is not maintained.

14-B. HUSKEY GAP TRAIL. Leaves No. 14 about 8.5 mi. from A.T.; leads left 2.5 mi. to public road 1 mi. S of Elkmont. Lower 1 mi. is on fire-road, which is open to motor travel May through October.

14.-C. HUSKEY GAP TRAIL. Leaves No. 14 about 8.5 mi. from A.T.; leads right 2.6 mi. to Newfound Gap Rd.

15. NOLAND DIVIDE TRAIL. Leaves Skyway 0.5 mi. W of Collins Gap and about 1.5 mi. from Forney Ridge parking area; leads S 11.1 mi. to public road at Deep Creek Ranger Station via crest of Noland Divide for 9 mi., thence down Juney Whank Branch to Deep Creek.

The first 2 mi. is through virgin spruce; remainder, through virgin oak. Lower end passes through rough, rocky terrain.

15-A. UPPER SASSAFRAS GAP TRAIL. Leaves No. 15 at Upper Sassafras Gap, 3.1 mi. S of A.T.; leads left 4 mi. to Bryson Place on Deep Creek.

15-B. NOLAND CREEK TRAIL. Leaves No. 15 at Upper Sassafras Gap, 3.1 mi. S of A.T.; leads right 3.5 mi. to dead end road on Noland Creek. This is not a standard trail.

16. CLINGMANS DOME TRAIL. Leaves A.T. 50 yd. E of summit of Clingmans Dome; leads 50 yd. to tower and thence on a paved path 0.5 mi. downhill to Forney Ridge parking area at end of Skyway, 7.6 mi. from Newfound Gap.

17. FORNEY RIDGE TRAIL. Leaves A.T. 0.4 mi. W of Clingmans Dome; leads 12.5 mi. to Fontana Lake. (Public road on Forney Creek and N.C. 288, which formerly afforded access to Bryson City, is now inundated.) Affords marvelous views of Forney Creek and Noland Creek valleys. At 2.5 mi. cross Andrews Bald, example of famous balds with its large mountain meadow. At lower end of meadow, turn sharp right. Variable spring is on lower end (SW corner) of Andrews Bald.

17-A. FORNEY CREEK TRAIL. Leaves No. 17 at 1.5 mi. S of A.T.; leads right 10.8 mi. via Forney Creek to Fontana Lake. Last 8.2 mi. is on fire-road.

17-B. BOARD CAMP TRAIL. Leaves No. 17 at 6.5 mi. S of A.T.; leads right 2.2 mi. to Forney Creek fire-road and 5.5 mi. farther to Fontana Lake.

17-C. SPRINGHOUSE BRANCH TRAIL. Leaves No. 17 at 6.5 mi. of A.T.; leads left 2.8 mi. to dead-end road on Noland Creek.

18. GOSHEN PRONG TRAIL. Leaves A.T. 0.8 mi. E of Double Springs Gap; leads N 10 mi. to public road, 1 mi. S of Elkmont. The first 0.2 mi. is through spruce; 1.2 mi. is through rhododendron and hemlock; balance is through cutover land rapidly recovering with hardwoods. The last 3 mi. is on fire-road along Little River, which is open to motor travel May through October. Trail is classified as ''manway.''

19. WELCH RIDGE TRAIL. Leaves A.T. 0.2 mi. E of Silers Bald; leads
S 8 mi. to High Rocks firetower. Follows crest of Welch Ridge to
High Rocks. Traverses second-growth hardwoods and offers views of
adjacent valleys with outstanding vantage point at High Rocks
firetower.

   19-A. JONAS CREEK TRAIL. Leaves No. 19 at 2.5 mi. S of A.T.;
   leads left 4 mi. to Forney Creek fire-road and 4.5 mi. farther to
   Fontana Lake. Follows Yanu Ridge and Jonas and Forney
   Creeks.

   19-B. JUMP-UP RIDGE TRAIL. Leaves No. 19 at 6.4 mi. S of
   A.T.; leads left 7.4 mi. to Fontana Lake. Last 3. 8 mi. is on
   Bear Creek and Forney Creek fire-roads. Follows Jump-up
   Ridge and Bear and Forney Creeks.

20. MIRY RIDGE TRAIL. Leaves A.T. 0.1 mi. W of Buckeye Gap;
leads N 9.2 mi. to public road at Elkmont. Follows Miry Ridge and
Dripping Springs Mtn. to Jakes Gap and thence down Jakes Creek;
lower end is on fire-road.

   20-A. LYNN CAMP PRONG TRAIL. Leaves No. 20 at 2.5 mi. N of
   A.T.; leads left 8 mi. to public road on Middle Prong Little
   River above Tremont Ranger Station. Lower end is on fire-
   road, 3.5 mi. of which is open to motor travel May through
   October. Large laurel is seen on this trail. Trail is classified as
   "manway."

   20-B. BLANKET MTN. TRAIL. Leaves No. 20 at Jakes Gap, 5.2
   mi. N of A.T.; leads ahead 0.8 mi. to Blanket Mtn.

   20-C. PANTHER CREEK TRAIL. Leaves No. 20 at Jakes Gap 5.2
   mi. N of A.T.; leads left 2.5 mi. to fire-road on Lynn Camp
   Prong above Tremont Ranger Station.

21. GREENBRIER RIDGE TRAIL. Leaves A.T. 0.2 mi. E of Derrick
Knob Shelter; leads N 8 mi. to public road on Middle Prong Little
River above Tremont Ranger Station. Route is through beech woods
for 0.2 mi., and then in cutover area. Lower end is on fire-road, 3.5
mi. of which is open to motor travel May through October.

22. JENKINS RIDGE TRAIL. Leaves A.T. at E end of Spence Field;
leads 7.5 mi. to fire-road at Flint Spring Gap.

23. BOTE MTN. TRAIL. Leaves A.T. near center of Spence Field; leads N 6.6 mi. to Cades Cove Rd. on Laurel Creek. First 0.5 mi. is through beech and birch forest; 0.5 mi., through laurel and hemlock; 1 mi., laurel slick; balance, on fire-road, through pine and hardwoods.

    23-A. ANTHONY CREEK TRAIL. Leaves No. 23 at 1.6 mi. N of A.T.; leads left through hardwood forest 3.4 mi. to public road in E end of Cades Cove. Lower end is on fire-road.

    23-B. FODDERSTACK MTN. TRAIL. Leaves No. 23 at 5.5 mi. S of A.T.; leads right 2.8 mi. to public road on Middle Prong Little River, above Tremont Ranger Station.

24. EAGLE CREEK TRAIL. Leaves A.T. near center of Spence Field; leads S 9 mi. to Fontana Lake.

25. LEADBETTER RIDGE TRAIL. Leaves A.T. at Russell Field; leads N 5.5 mi. to public road in E end of Cades Cove. First 0.5 mi. is across grassy bald, ungraded but marked; then 0.5 mi., through virgin hardwood forest; 1 mi., on pine ridge (Leadbetter Ridge); then down Right Prong of Anthony Creek and Anthony Creek, through beautiful forest of hemlock and rhododendron. Growth here is so dense and moss-covered it gives tropical effect. Lower end is on fire-road.

26. GREGORY BALD TRAIL. Leaves A.T. at Doe Knob; leads right 7.5 mi. to Parson Branch Rd. (open to one-way traffic from Cades Cove to U.S. 129 May through October). Route from Doe Knob to Sheep Pen Gap is portion of former A.T. in western Great Smokies, which was abandoned when A.T. was relocated to cross Little Tennessee River at Fontana Dam. At 2.9 mi. from A.T., Gregory Bald (4,948 ft.) is of special interest in late June because of its outstanding display of azalea. The bald comprises about 200 acres and affords fine panoramic view. Cherokee Indians called this bald "Tsistuyi," the "rabbit place," where the chief of the rabbits ruled. It was bald when settlers first came. They grazed sheep on it. Since establishment of Great Smoky Mtns. National Park and end of grazing, the bald has become overgrown, diminishing impression of cleared, open fields, and somewhat restricting view.

    26-A. HUNGRY RIDGE TRAIL. Leaves No. 26 at Rich Gap (also known as "Gant Lot," the mountaineers' name for a locality where cattle were corralled to be ''hardened up'' or ''gaunted . . . ga'nted'' before being driven from the mountains); leads S 8 mi. to N.C. 28, 3.7 mi. from Deals Gap on U.S. 129. Follows Long Hungry Ridge, Rye Patch Branch, and Twenty-mile Creek. Lower 3.3 mi. is on fire-road.

26-B. GREGORY RIDGE TRAIL. Leaves No. 26 at Rich Gap; leads N 4.5 mi. to public road near W end of Cades Cove. Follows Gregory Ridge for about 2.2 mi. and then descends and follows Ekaneetlee Branch and Forge Creek. On ridge it passes through hardwoods and pine; and upon reaching branch, through some of largest poplars and hemlocks in Park.

26-C. PARSON BALD TRAIL. Leaves No. 26 at 3.3 mi. from A.T.; leads left about 0.8 mi. to Parson Bald, peak similar to Gregory Bald but smaller.

27. SHUCKSTACK TRAIL. Leaves A.T. at Sassafras Gap, 0.5 mi. N of Shuckstack firetower; leads right 5.2 mi. to N.C. 28, 3.7 mi. from Deals Gap on U.S. 129. Follows Proctor Branch and Twenty-mile Creek. Lower 3.3 mi. is on fire-road.

Mountain
Laurel

THE A.T. IN THE NANTAHALA NATIONAL FOREST

(From the Little Tennessee River to the North Carolina-Georgia State Line)

Distance 88.6 Miles

The Appalachian Trail through the Nantahala National Forest is routed through mature, hardwood forest for the most part. The growth of rhododendron, mountain laurel, flame azalea, mountain ash, the vast beds of fern and galax, the ever-changing profusion of wildflower blooming from April to frost, the frequent streams and springs, and the fall coloring, all contribute to make the A.T. in the south so distinctive.

The Rev. A. Rufus Morgan, who helped establish and maintain the A.T. in North Carolina, has described the area most eloquently:

". . . A trip in October will give opportunity of seeing grouse, wild turkeys, squirrels, deer, and occasionally other wild life. The coloring, also, makes a fall trip a beautiful experience. Early October will give an abundance of wildflowers, such as asters, phlox, self-heal, and closed gentian.

"A spring trip, perhaps in late April, will show the white flowering trees, such as dogwood, bellwood, service, and black locust. Along with these the red maples show a beautiful contrast. Then there are the flowers . . . the bluets furnish quite a carpet. There are violets in abundance, as well as the trilliums and trout lilies. The many varieties of fern present an interesting study . . . from Deep Gap to the Georgia line the interrupted fern grows in great profusion . . . during June (and July) . . . a wealth of flame azalea and rhododendron, especially the purple rhododendron on Standing Indian Mtn."

The A.T. route through the Nantahala National Forest offers many opportunities for short and long hikes. Specifics are included under each section of Trail which follows.

Generally, it may be useful to point out the many recreational facilities and historical importance of the area around Fontana Dam, the northernmost part of the A.T. in the NNF. (Details are in Section 3.)

A most rewarding trip from Fontana is to the Joyce Kilmer Memorial Forest. Driving distance is 21.7 mi. from the intersection of U.S. 129 with N.C. 28. The forest is a reservation of magnificent and inspiring trees. An easy trail of about 1½ mi. leads past the Kilmer Memorial through superlative forest growth. Overnight camping is not permitted. However, the USFS Horse Cove Campground is adjacent.

Trails to three outstanding mountains begin in the Joyce Kilmer Forest. These are Hangover Mtn., (5,160 ft.) Haoe (5,249 ft.), and Stratton Bald (5,341 ft.). For trails to Hangover and Snowbird Mtns., see TVA Tapoco and Santeetlah Creek quadrangles and USFS Nantahala National Forest Map. Also of much interest is the Snowbird Range to the S. See Nantahala National Forest Map.

In general, the first part of the A.T. route parallels the Little Tennessee River. It heads E from near the W end of the Great Smokies to the N end of the Nantahala Range. Particularly impressive are the panoramic views of the Great Smokies on one side and the Nantahala, Cowee, and Snowbird Mtns. on the other. The view from Cheoah Bald is one of the outstanding views of the Southern Appalachians.

At the Nantahala River, the A.T. climbs out of Nantahala Gorge and proceeds over a series of 5,000-ft. summits (the heath balds so characteristic of the Southern Applachians) and 4,000-ft. gaps. It flanks the headwaters of the Nantahala, Little Tennessee, and Tallulah Rivers. At Ridgepole Mtn., the end of the Nantahala Range, it turns to the Blue Ridge for the rest of its journey to Georgia.

The Appalachian Trail goes through historic country in western North Carolina. Before the coming of white settlers in the 18th Century, the entire area was inhabited by the Cherokee Nation, with settlements along all the major streams and trails going through the gaps. Hernando de Soto is known to have traveled from Nikwasi (the present-day Franklin) across the Nantahalas to the site of Murphy in 1539. He must have gone through one of the gaps along the route of the Appalachian Trail. In 1775, the naturalist William Bartram, traveled the Indian trail from Nikwasi to the Nantahala River, hoping to reach the Overhill towns in East Tennessee. The following year, General Rutherford, on a search-and-destroy mission against the Cherokee Indians, led his troups through Wayah Gap, and fought a skirmish there. In 1819 a line separating Cherokee and white settlements was drawn along the crest of the Nantahalas. ''Old 64'' in Wallace Gap follows the route of one of the Indian trading paths that developed into a colonial road. Siler Bald in the Nantahalas was named for an early settler, William Siler, whose great-grandson, the Rev. A. Rufus Morgan, helped establish the A.T. in North Carolina. Albert Mtn. was named for Dr.

Morgan's grandfather, Albert Siler. Standing Indian Campground, situated on the headwaters of the Nantahala River, was the site of a lumber camp in the late 19th and early 20th centuries. The John B. Byrne observation tower (memorial to the former supervisor of the Nantahala National Forest who first proposed the route of the Appalachian Trail in this area) is located on Wayah Bald.

Recent relocations of the A.T. logging operations in the National Forest, and a two-year drought have all had their impact on the bubbling springs and pure mountain streams of the southern mountains. Hikers are urged to carry an emergency supply of drinking water with them at all times, and to boil any drinking water found along the Trail or in the shelters.

Camping is permitted almost everywhere in the National Forest (prohibited areas are clearly marked by USFS signs); it is not necessary to register for the 8 shelters along the route.

The section of A.T. from the Little Tennessee River to the Nantahala River (Wesser) is maintained by members of the Smoky Mountains Hiking Club. The sections from the Nantahala River (Wesser) to Bly Gap (the North Carolina-Georgia State Line) are maintained by members of the Nantahala Hiking Club.

Most of the A.T. is in the Wayah District, Nantahala National Forest whose office is in Franklin, N.C.; the Deep Gap-Bly Gap section is the Tusquittee District, office in Murphy, N.C. (Trail maintenance is also provided by USFS personnel.)

This chapter has been divided into eight sections. Each section has introductory material which describes the terrain, the approaches, side trails, water sources, campsites, etc. Each section also has a summary of detailed Trail data, with N-S and S-N mileages listed separately. The chapter concludes with a special section: *Side Trails in the Nantahalas*. The eight sections are the following:

LITTLE TENNESSEE RIVER (FONTANA DAM) TO YELLOW CREEK GAP

Distance 8.1 miles

Brief Description of Section

The A.T. originally extended the length of the Great Smokies and utilized the only available crossing of the Little Tennessee River at Tapoco, N.C. From that point, the Yellow Creek Mtns. were followed E for 12.7 mi. to Yellow Creek Gap.

In 1946 Fontana Dam and the development of Fontana Village, with its opportunities as a recreational and mountain climbing center, made feasible the crossing of the Little Tennessee River at Fontana Dam.

The initial location and marking of the Trail in this area were accomplished in 1932-33 by the Smoky Mountains Hiking Club.

From Fontana Dam, for about 0.8 mi., the route is a hard-surfaced highway toward Fontana Village, then a ridgecrest through woods to Fontana Boat Dock parking area. From N.C. 28, at the boat dock parking area, the USFS, in 1971, relocated the A.T. to ascend via Bee Cove Lead to Walker Gap on Yellow Creek Mtn., a change in elevation of about 1,650 feet in 2.6 mi. It then heads E along Yellow Creek Mtn. to rejoin the former Trail route at Black Gum Gap.

Points of Interest

Fontana Dam, part of the TVA system, was constructed on the Little Tennessee River during the war to furnish hydroelectric power. The dam is 480 ft. high, the highest in Eastern America. The powerhouse and penstock are at the bottom near the center of the river channel. An inclined railway leads from the powerhouse to the visitors' building at the top of the dam. The dam impounded the Little Tennessee River for 29 mi. to create Fontana Lake, thus making the southern boundary of the adjacent Great Smoky Mountains National Park a water boundary.

In May, 1946, Fontana Village, which was constructed at Welch Cove to house TVA construction workers, was transferred to Government Services, Inc., for operation as a public recreation area. The village is 3 mi.

from the dam at an elevation of 1,800 ft., immediately at the base of the Yellow Creek Mtns. Extensive facilities are available here, including a lodge, cafeteria, drug store, grocery store, post office, laundry, and medical center. About 300 houses, which were used in the construction, constitute the available accommodations.

Government Services, Inc., has a very extensive recreation program under the direction of a recreational supervisor. Hiking, fishing, and horseback trips are featured.

The dam project, which created the lake with a normal shore line elevation of about 1,710 ft., flooded out N.C. 288 from Deals Gap to Bryson City. A hard-surfaced road, N.C. 28, leads from U.S. 129 to Fontana Dam (9.5 mi from Deals Gap) and continues to a junction with U.S. 19 about 9 mi. S of Bryson City.

Farther down the Little Tennessee River is Cheoah Dam, which is just above the bridge utilized by the former A.T. route. The dam is 200 ft. high and backs up the river for about 6 mi. Below is Calderwood Lake, made by the Calderwood Dam, farther down river.

Road Approaches

The N end of this Trail section crosses N.C. 28 about 0.8 mi. from Fontana Dam and about 2 mi. E of Fontana Village.

In Yellow Creek Gap the Trail crosses the Yellow Creek Mtn. Rd. 8.14 mi. S of Fontana Dam. Four miles to the E of this crossing is N.C. 28. To the W, about 10 mi., is N.C. 129.

There is no longer bus service to Fontana. Hikers may arrange to ride with the mail carrier between Maryville and Fontana. Written inquiries should be sent to Henry Morrow, 1225 Hutton St., Maryville, Tenn. 37801.

Maps

See TVA Fontana Dam quadrangle. For map of Fontana Village, ask for Fontana Village Location Map from Government Services, Inc., Fontana Dam, N.C. 28733.

Shelters, Campsites, and Water

Fontana Dam Shelter is located in the TVA Complex at Fontana Dam.

Cable Gap Shelter is located 7.3 mi. from the N end of this section. Sources of water are infrequent, and in dry seasons even well-recognized and publicized sources of water may fail. Ample provision for water should be made.

The USFS also maintains the Horse Cove Campground, adjacent to the Joyce Kilmer Memorial Forest; and camping is permitted in the slickrock portion of the wilderness area.

Public Accommodations

Fontana Village, 2 mi. W of the A.T. on N.C. 28, is an excellent source of supplies, with a general store and post office. In Robbinsville, N.C., 8.6 mi. W on Sweetwater Rd., accommodations are available (by reservation) at the Snowbird Mountain Lodge.

Trail Description, North to South

Miles	Data
0.0	From the N bank of the Little Tennessee River follow the roadway across the dam.
0.4	Reach the S bank. On the right at S abutment of dam are visitors' buildings with exhibits explaining the operation of the dam, refreshment stand (closed in winter), rest rooms, public showers, and access to passenger cable car down to powerhouse. Ascend on hard-surface road.
0.9	At crest of ridge pass parking overlook on left which affords good views of Fontana Lake to the Great Smokies. There is also a picnic area with *water* fountains and rest rooms (closed in winter). Descend on hard-surface road.
1.0	Bear left onto Trail into woods, and continue along curving ridgecrest, ascending and descending gently. Descend to hard-surface road at swimming pool, bear left and cross road. At the top of rise where hard surface road drops steeply to boat docks, bear to right around concrete comfort stations (closed in winter) and ascend on grassy slope and stone steps to N.C. 28.
1.7	Reach highway. Fontana Village is about 2 mi. to the right. Cross road and ascend stone steps. Ascend gradually along narrow ridge crest.
2.1	Bear right at head of draw and then turn sharp right.
2.5	*Water* is to right immediately below Trail.
3.0	Pass through Gap and turn sharp right along Bee Cove Lead. Ascend along right side of ridgecrest.
3.4	Turn sharp left.
3.5	Pass rock cliffs on the right.
3.6	Regain crest of Bee Cove Lead and turn sharp right, ascending steeply along crest.
4.0	Trail bears right from Bee Cove Lead.
4.2	Trail crosses *stream*.
4.3	Trail crosses another *stream* and bears left.
4.4	Reach Walker Gap at 3,450 ft. on the crest of Yellow Creek Mtn. Note trail intersection. Fontana Village is about 2.7 mi. by Yellow Creek Mtn. and Lookout Rock Trails. Turn left along A.T.

5.1   Cross high point with rocks on summit at 3,720 ft.
5.2   Cross another high point, descend and continue along crest, ascending and descending.
5.9   Pass through Black Gum Gap.
6.2   With High Top (highest point on Yellow Creek Mtn. at 3,786 ft.) ahead leave the ridgecrest and skirt the right side.
6.5   Bear S to switchback; then, bear left along S slope, descending toward Cable Gap with *Cable Gap Shelter* visible ahead. Descend with views to the S.
7.1   Turn sharp right, downhill.
7.9   Turn sharp left with *Cable Gap Shelter* on the right. This shelter was built in 1939 by the CCC under the direction of the Nantahala National Forest. *Spring* is adjacent. At S side of shelter at steps, Trail through Cable Gap to Yellow Creek Rd. continues about 0.1 mi. downhill. From the shelter ascend, climbing S slope of pointed Tommy Knob.
8.1   Reach road intersection in Yellow Creek Gap at 2,960 ft. To left it is 4 mi to N.C. 28, where there are several motels near the intersection. Fontana Village is about 9 mi. to left on N.C. 28, a total of 13 mi. from Yellow Creek Gap. The A.T. continues directly opposite up stone steps into woods.

Trail Description, South to North

Miles   **Data**

0.0   From the Yellow Creek Rd. at the crest of ridge (2,980 ft.) proceed along left side of ridge.
0.4   Start descent into Cable Gap.
0.9   Pass the *Cable Gap Shelter* on the left. This shelter was built in 1939 by the CCC for the Nantahala Forest Service. A trail to the left leads about 0.4 mi. down to the Yellow Creek Rd.
1.0   Turn sharp left, climbing S side of High Top. This peak at 3,786 ft. is the highest point on the Yellow Creek Range, but dense growth precludes any views. Ascend the S slope where the Yellow Creek Valley can be seen.
1.7   Switch back and bear N along a spur of High Top.
2.0   Reach the crest of the ridge where Fontana Lake can be seen to the right. Continue W along the main crest.

2.1   Pass a worn trail on right in a slight sag.

2.6   Pass through Black Gum Gap and continue along crest ascending and descending.

2.8   Cross high point of ridgecrest.

3.0   Cross another high point with rocks on the summit at 3,720 ft.

3.7   Reach Walker Gap at 3,450 ft. and note trail intersection. (Fontana Village is about 2.7 mi. straight ahead by the Yellow Creek Mtn. Trail and Lookout Rock Trail.) Turn right on the A.T. and descend.

3.8   Trail bears right.

3.9   Cross small *stream*

4.0   Cross another larger *stream*.

4.6   Trail bears left along ridge crest, Bee Cove Lead.

4.4   Descend steeply.

4.5   Trail turns sharp to left.

4.7   Pass rock cliffs on the left and turn right.

5.1   Pass through gap, turn sharp left leaving Bee Cove Lead.

5.7   *Water* is to left immediately below Trail.

6.0   Come onto ridgecrest and bear left.

6.3   Reach N.C. 28. (Fontana Village is about 2 mi. to left.) Cross road and immediately descend stone steps and turn right down grassy slope. Pass a concrete comfort station on the right (closed in winter) and reach hard-surface road. Turn left along road toward swimming pool and enter woods to right. Ascend to ridge crest, and follow Trail ascending and descending gently.

7.6   Reach hard-surface road and continue toward Fontana Dam.

7.2   Pass picnic area on the right and descend along highway to the dam.

7.8   Reach the S end of the dam. (On left are visitors' buildings with exhibits explaining operation of the dam, refreshment stand which is closed in winter, rest rooms, public showers, and access to passenger cable car down to powerhouse.)

8.1   Reach the N bank of the Little Tennessee River by crossing dam.

YELLOW CREEK GAP TO STECOAH GAP

Distance 7.6 miles

Brief Description of Section

The A.T. crosses Yellow Creek Rd. at the crest of Yellow Creek Gap (2,960 ft.). Stone steps lead into the woods. From here the A.T. begins a long ascent to Cody Gap, a similar distance along the crest and then a steep descent to Brown Fork Gap. The Trail resumes a steep ascent, levels off a bit and begins a long descent to Sweetwater Gap. Another up and down climb brings the hiker to Stecoah Gap.

Points of Interest

Excellent views of Cheoah Bald and a side trail to Wauchecha Bald highlight this section of A.T. The Trail formerly went to the summit of Wauchecha (4,385 ft.) but that route is now part of a loop trail of less than a 1-mi. distance.

Road Approaches

In Yellow Creek Gap the A.T. crosses the Yellow Creek Mtn. Rd. (hard-surface) 8.1 mi. S of Fontana Dam. Four mi. E of this crossing is N.C. 28. To the W, N.C. 129 is about 10 mi.

In Stecoah Gap, 12.3 mi. N of Wesser, the Trail crosses the Sweetwater Creek Rd. N.C. 28 is about 3 mi. to the E.

Maps

TVA Fontana Dam and Hewitt quadrangles.

Shelters, Campsites, and Water

There are no shelters on this section. Water is available near Cody Gap, Brown Fork Gap, Sweetwater Gap, and Stecoah Gap. However, in dry seasons, water sources may not be available.

Public Accommodations

From Stecoah Gap, it is 8.6 mi. on a hard-surface road to Robbinsville, where public accommodations are available.

Trail Description, North to South

Miles	Data
0.0	From road intersection at crest of Yellow Creek Gap ascend stone steps and enter woods on Trail. Bear to right of ridgecrest ascending.
0.4	Cross *stream* at foot of small cascade.
1.4	Reach main ridgecrest and bear right.
1.6	Cross knob which affords excellent view of Cheoah Bald to left.
1.7	Bear right from ridgecrest.
2.4	Regain ridgecrest and bear right along crest. Reach Cody Gap. (The Trail to right, former A.T. route, leads about 200 yds. to *water*.) Bear left on Trail out of Gap. (Trail straight ahead, uphill, is former A.T. route and is now a part of the Wauchecha Bald Loop Trail. It is about 0.9 mi. to Wauchecha Bald at 4,385 ft. where there is a firetower.) Continue on Trail with little elevation change around the side of Cheoah Mtn.
3.2	Pass through Hogback Gap and ascend to knob at 3,912 ft. Turn left (E) along ridge crest and descend.
4.9	Pass through Brown Fork Gap. Ascend slightly.
5.1	Enter gap where *water* can be found 35 yds. to the left. Ascend slightly.
5.2	Enter gap where *water* can be found 70 yds. to the left.
5.6	Reach crest of narrow ridge which Trail follows descending, in S course.
5.8	Pass cliffs, 15 yd. to right, which affords excellent views of the Snowbird Mtns. Descend steeply.
6.6	Pass through Sweetwater Gap. *Water* is 0.13 mi. down W (right) slope. Ascend.
6.8	Reach crest of ridge and descend gradually.
7.5	Reach hard-surface road leading to Stecoah Gap. Ascend.
7.6	Reach Stecoah Gap at 3,165 ft. (There is a good spring about 0.1 mi. to the right and downhill on a logging road. About 8.6 mi. to the right on hard-surface road accommodations are available in Robbinsville.)

Trail Description, South to North

Miles	Data
0.0	From the crest of road in Stecoah Gap descend gradually to right to where Trail leaves hard-surface road.
0.2	Leave road and ascend to crest of ridge.
0.4	Reach crest of ridge and ascend steeply.
0.8	Reach the top of ridge and descend steeply to Sweetwater Gap. *Water* is 0.13 mi. to the left in gap.
1.0	Pass through Sweetwater Gap and ascend steeply to rock cliffs.
1.9	Reach cliffs, 15 yd. to left, which afford splendid views of the Snowbird Mtns.
2.1	Reach crest of narrow ridge then gradually descend into gap.
2.4	Pass through gap where *water* can be found 70 yd. to the right. Ascend slightly.
2.5	Pass through gap where *water* can be found 35 yd. to the right. Ascend knob.
2.7	Trail passes through Brown Fork Gap and makes a series of small ascents and descents.
3.3	Reach the crest of knob where outstanding views are afforded. Descend into Hogback Gap.
4.4	In Hogback Gap bear right on Trail. (The Trail uphill is the former A.T. route which is now a Blue Blaze Loop Trail to Wauchecha Bald.) Continue, with little change in elevation around the side of Cheoah Mtn.
5.2	Come into Cody Gap. (The Trail uphill is former A.T. route and is now a part of the Wauchecha Bald Loop Trail. (Wauchecha Bald [4,385 ft.] is located 0.9 mi. from Cody Gap. There is a USFS firetower there which affords excellent views. The Trail to the left in Cody Gap is the former A.T. route which leads approximately 200 yd. to *water*.) From Cody Gap bear right along the ridgecrest.
5.6	Bear left away from crest.
5.9	Rejoin ridgecrest and bear left along crest.
6.0	Cross knob which affords excellent view of Cheoah Bald to right.
6.2	Bear left away from ridge crest.

7.2   Cross stream at foot of small cascade and descend into Yellow Creek Gap.

7.6   Reach Yellow Creek Gap (2,960 ft.). (Hard-surface road to the right leads to N.C. 28 where there are several motels near the intersection. Fontana Village is about 13 mi. from the gap along N.C. 28.) The A.T. continues directly opposite, across the main road.

SECTION 5

STECOAH GAP TO THE NANTAHALA RIVER (WESSER)

Distance 13.1 Miles

Brief Description of Section

This section of A.T. involves the steep ascent and descent of Cheoah Bald (5,062 ft.). Switchbacks and small knobs along the crests are prevalent. The A.T. crosses the Nantahala River at the S end of this section, winding up opposite the Wesser Railroad Station, on the road from the station to U.S. 19.

Points of Interest

At the summit of Cheoah Bald, a brief side trail leads to a lookout point. The views from Cheoah are among the greatest in the Southern Appalachians. Also worth noting are the rock formations of ''Nantahala Slate'' that form a knife edge S of the Cheoah summit. Farther S, the A.T. route offers good views of the Nantahala Gorge and proceeds through a beautiful hardwood cove on its descent to Wesser.

Road Approaches

On the N end, the A.T. crosses Sweetwater Creek Rd. at Stecoah Gap. N.C. 28 is about 3 mi. to the E.

The S end is at U.S. 19 in Wesser. Carolina Trailways buses (Asheville to Chattanooga) operate through Wesser. The town is on the Murphy

Division of Southern Railroad from Asheville. Bryson City, N.C., is 1 mi. NE on U.S. 19; Murphy, N.C., is 38 mi. S.

Maps

TVA Hewitt and Wesser and quadrangles, and USFS Nantahala National Forest Map.

Shelters, Campsites, and Water

The Sassafras Gap Trail Shelter is located almost midway along this section, about 120 yd. off the A.T.

There are a campsite and spring S of the summit of Swim Bald.

The A. Rufus Morgan Shelter is 0.8 mi. S of Wesser.

While there are usually many fine springs and sources of water along this section, hikers are encouraged to carry their own during dry seasons.

Public Accommodations

There are a motel, restaurant, and store at Wesser. The Nantahala Outdoor Center (Wesser) is an excellent supply point. Packages may be mailed there.

From Wesser, it is 15 mi. NE to Bryson City, N.C., on U.S. 19.

From Stecoah Gap, it is 8.6 mi. to Robbinsville, where public accommodations are available.

Trail Description, North to South

Miles	Data
0.0	From road at crest of Stecoah Gap follow Trail up steps to left of ridge crest ascending S gradually through a series of switchbacks.
0.7	Reach high point of ridge, turn right and pass over a series of small knobs along crest.
2.1	Pass through Simp Gap. Ascend and follow Trail over a series of small knobs.
3.0	Pass through Locust Cove Gap. *Water* is located 150 yd. to the right. *Spring* is variable. Follow Trail to right leading out of gap ascending gradually to ridgecrest.
3.4	Reach ridgecrest and turn sharp to the left.
3.8	Reach old A.T. junction, and follow Trail to the right.

5.1	Turn sharp left. The Trail to right leads to Bellcollar and Bear Creek. Ascend to the summit of Cheoah Bald.
5.3	Reach the summit of Cheoah Bald (5,062 ft.). Fantastic views are to be had here. (Trail to left leads to lookout point.) From the summit descend S along knife edge of blue ''Nantahala Slate.''
5.4	Turn sharp left (E) and descend gradually, then more steeply into Sassafras Gap.
6.3	Pass through Sassafras Gap. *Spring* is 20 yd. to the left and 100 yd. to the right. *Sassafras Gap Trail Shelter* is approximately 120 yd. on Trail to right and downhill from the *spring*. From the gap ascend along the N side of knob then descend.
6.6	Cross gap and ascend toward summit of Swim Bald.
7.2	Reach summit of Swim Bald (4,720 ft.). Care should be exercised at this point. Bear somewhat to the S, and go onto main ridge. Another ridge extends from Swim Bald down to N and is often confused with the one running almost directly E. There is a variable *spring* approximately 250 yd. E of summit of Swim Bald to left. There is a fine *campsite* near the *spring* which lies in a grassy notch, where the E ridge (A.T.) and N ridge converge. In extremely dry weather it may be necessary to go as much as ½ mi. down *stream*, which parallels the Trail, to find *water*. Descending along the ridge which the A.T. follows are good views of the Nantahala Gorge. This ridge becomes exceedingly sharp, especially on the S slope.
8.3	Trail turns very sharply to the left and gently descends into a beautiful hardwood cove.
8.8	Trail switches back sharply to the right and descends gradually into gap, passing a *spring* affording reliable *water*.
9.3	Come into gap and continue along ridgecrest.
9.6	Come onto ridgecrest and descend along side of ridge.
10.8	Reach Grassy Gap (3,050 ft.). Bear right along worn Trail around side of Tyre Top.
10.6	Pass through sag. Trail to right leads about 100 yd. to *spring*.
10.7	Reach crest of ridge running S from Tyre Top (3,760 ft.). Bear right, descending along ridgecrest.
11.4	Reach dirt road at Wright Gap. Cross road and ascend to ridge crest.

11.7	Cross under power line and follow Trail along side of Flint Ridge.
12.8	Reach ridge spur and descend gradually to railroad track.
13.0	Reach railroad tracks, turn left and follow tracks to bridge crossing Nantahala River. Cross bridge.
13.1	Reach E bank of Nantahala River and end of section at U.S. 19 in Wesser. (The Wesser Creek Lean-to is 3.0 mi. from the end of this section, at the base of Wesser Bald.)

Trail Description, South to North

Miles   **Data**

0.0	Leave highway at E bank of Nantahala River, cross bridge and turn left up railroad track.
0.1	Leave railroad track and take Trail to right gradually ascending to ridge spur.
0.7	Reach crest of ridge spur and follow Trail along side of Flint Ridge.
1.4	Cross under powerline.
1.7	Descend to dirt road at Wright Gap. Cross road and make steep ascent of ridge to Tyre Top.
2.3	Near the base of Tyre Top take left to skirt the SE side of Tyre Top (3,760 ft.).
2.5	Descend into sag. The Trail to left leads about 100 yd. to *spring*.
2.9	Reach Grassy Gap (3,050 ft.), ascend and skirt E side of ridge.
3.5	Reach crest of Grassy Top and descend into gap.
3.7	From gap, Trail turns to right and gradually ascends into a beautiful hardwood cove passing a reliable *spring*.
4.2	Trail switches back sharply to the left and gradually ascends to knife-edge of rock, which affords spectacular views.
5.4	*Water* is about 100 yd. downhill to the right.
5.7	Variable *spring* is about 50 yd. to right. It lies in a grassy notch, where the E ridge (A.T.) and the N ridge converge; fine campsite here. This *spring* and those at Sassafras Gap and Tyre Top constitute the only sure sources of water between Stecoah Gap and Wesser.

.9   Reach summit of Swim Bald, bear slightly to the right and descend. On the opposite side is a splended view of the Smokies.

5.4   Cross gap, proceed along right side of knob.

.8   Descend into Sassafras Gap. *Springs* are 20 yd. to the right and 100 yd. to left. The *Sassafras Gap Shelter* is about 120 yd. on the trail to left and downhill from the spring. From this gap, climb toward Cheoah Bald, known as Beech Creek Bald locally. Ascent is steep at first, then more gradual.

7.7   Reach crest of ridge, turn sharp right, uphill and ascend along knife-edge of blue ''Nantahala Slate'' to the triangulation station at Cheoah Bald.

7.8   Reach the summit of Cheoah Bald (5,062 ft.). (This peak affords one of the most splendid panoramas in the Southern Appalachians. Trail to the right leads to the lookout point for striking view of the Great Smokies.) A.T. bears left. Descent is gradual.

7.9   Turn sharp right from the descending ridge. This is an important turn. Caution! Trail directly ahead leads to Bellcollar Gap and Bear Creek.

9.3   Reach old A.T. junction. Follow Trail to left, gradually descending around the side and over the ridge spur into Locust Cove Gap.

0.1   Pass through Locust Cove Gap. Trail to left leads about 150 yd. to a variable *spring*. Trail leads to the left out of the gap switching back to ridgecrest.

0.3   Come back to ridgecrest and follow Trail over a series of small knobs.

1.0   Pass through Simp Gap and ascend to high point of ridge.

2.3   Reach highest point of the ridge. Turn sharp to the left. Caution! Follow Trail on gradual descent on a series of switchbacks to Stecoah Gap.

13.1   Reach Stecoah Gap (3,165 ft.), on top of divide. (Good *spring* about 0.1 mi. sharp left on logging road. Robbinsville is located 8.6 mi. to left on hard-surface road, where accommodations are available.)

NANTAHALA RIVER (WESSER, N.C.) TO TELLICO GAP

Distance 7.7 Miles

Brief Description of Section

This section begins at Wesser, N.C., on U.S. 19, opposite the Nantahala River bridge, 15 mi. W of Bryson City and 38 mi. N of Murphy, N.C. The Trail climbs steeply from Wesser (1,723 ft.) over Wesser Bald (4,627 ft.) and then descends to Tellico Gap (3,850 ft.).

Points of Interest

A recent relocation provides a scenic climb along a narrow ridge, with drop-offs on either side. Wesser Bald has a magnificent view of the ranges beyond the Nantahala Gorge as far as the Great Smokies.

Road Approaches

Wesser, N.C. is on U.S. 19. Tellico Gap, the southern end of the section, can be reached by a gravel road, N.C. 1365, 4 mi. from N.C. 1310 linking U.S. 19 and U.S. 64.

Shelters and Water

The A. Rufus Morgan Shelter is 0.8 mi. S of Wesser (6.9 mi. N of Tellico Gap). The old Wesser Creek shelter and the trail leading from it to Wesser Bald have been designated a side trail.

Water is somewhat scarce, the only source being a stream at the shelter site and a spring 5 mi. S at the foot of Wesser Bald. There is no water in Tellico Gap.

Maps

USFS map of the Nantahala National Forest and the TVA Wesser quadrangle. (Recent relocations of the A.T. are not shown on these maps.)

Public Accommodations

Wesser contains a store, restaurant, motel, laundry and showers. The Nantahala Outdoor Center, trail outfitter and operator of canoeing and rafting facilities, is located in Wesser.

Trail Description, North to South

Miles	Data
0.0	A.T. begins on U.S. 19 in Wesser, opposite the bridge, and climbs immediately into the woods.
0.8	Enter clearing, site of *A. Rufus Morgan Shelter* with a *stream* on right of clearing.
1.1	A.T. bears L; logging rd. to Silvermine Creek bears R. Trail from here climbs through woods with occasional vistas on either side.
2.6	Switchbacks as A.T. climbs to narrow ridge crest.
3.8	View of Fontana Lake, after steep climb.
4.1	Reach wooden steps over rocks.
4.3	Reach "Jump Up" with a spectacular view of mountain ranges to N.
5.6	On ridgecrest, come to blue-blazed Wesser Creek Trail on left. (this is the old route of the A.T.; it is 5 mi. to Wesser.)
5.7	Turn sharply right to begin climb to Wesser Bald (4,627 ft.) The blue-blazed trail ahead leads 100 ft. to *spring*.
6.3	On a rocky ledge, the A.T. bears right, downhill. (Trail to remains of old firetower on Wesser Bald leads left.)
7.7	Begin descent into Tellico Gap (3,850 ft.). (A rough road to the firetower is on left; gravel road, 4 mi. to the state highway, is on right.) A.T. crosses Tellico Gap under a power line.

Flame
Azalea

Trail Description, South to North

Miles	Data
0.0	A.T. bears to left of the fireroad in Tellico Gap (3,850 ft.), and then ascends the W slope of Wesser Bald by graded trail.
1.4	On a rocky ledge, begin ascent of Wesser Bald (4,627 ft.). (Trail to remnants of old firetower on Wesser Bald bears right.)
2.0	Trail turns sharply left. A blue-blazed trail leads 100 ft., right turn, to *spring*.
2.1	A.T. continues along ridge crest. Blue-blazed Wesser Creek trail (old route of the A.T., 5 mi. to Wesser) bears R downhill.
3.4	Reach "Jump Up" with a spectacular view of mountain ranges to N.
3.9	View of Fontana Lake after steep descent.
4.8	Reach beginning of graded trail through woods.
5.1	Switchbacks as A.T. descends through woods.
6.6	A.T. bears R; logging rd. to Silvermine Creek is on the L.
6.9	Enter clearing with the *A. Rufus Morgan Shelter*. A *stream* is on the left of clearing.
7.7	Descend through rhododendron, cross several *streams*, to U.S. 19, directly across from the Nantahala River bridge. To continue on Trail, cross road.

TELLICO GAP TO WAYAH GAP

Distance 14.1 miles

Brief Description of Section

This section begins in Tellico Gap (3,850 ft.) where a power line crosses the area. The Trail is graded throughout and crosses a series of 5,000-ft. balds. It is fairly steep in some places.

Points of Interest

Wayah Bald (5,336 ft.) is an outstanding feature of this section with views of the surrounding mountains from Georgia to the Great Smokies. The observation tower has been restored and trees removed to maintain the area as a bald.

Road Approaches

Tellico Gap is accessible by automobile from a gravel road (N.C. 1365), 4 mi. from N.C. 1310 linking U.S. 19 and U.S. 64. N.C. 1310 also provides access to the A.T. in Burningtown Gap (by gravel road, 1397, from Kyle), and to Wayah Bald (USFS gravel road, 4 mi. from Wayah Gap to Wayah Bald); N.C. 1310 leads to U.S. 64 and Franklin, N.C., 16 mi. to W, and the nearest stores and motels in N.C. S of Wesser.

Maps

USFS map of the Nantahala National Forest and the TVA Wayah Bald and Wesser quadrangles. (Recent relocations are not shown on these maps.)

Shelters, Campsites, and Water

The Cold Spring Shelter is located on the A.T., 3.9 mi. S of Tellico Gap, 1.3 mi N of Burningtown Gap. Camping is no longer permitted at Wayah Bald. (The old observation tower, having been heavily vandalized, is now off-limits.) There are a latrine and trash cans near the parking area. Nearby is a USFS picnic area (no water). There is also a picnic area at Wayah Crest in Wayah Gap.

Water is available at Cold Spring Shelter, and at four streams along the route. The former water source at Wayah Crest has been dislocated by a new gravel road. There is no water at Wayah Bald.

Public Accommodations

There are no public accommodations or supplies at either end of this section.

Trail Description, North to South

Miles	Data
0.0	A.T. is a graded trail that crosses Tellico Gap (3,850 ft.) under a power line.
1.7	Reach campsite and *spring* on right, after steep climb. Cross in succession Rocky Bald, Black Bald, and Tellico Bald.
3.5	At Copper Bald (5,200 ft.), start descent from ridgecrest which has views of the Nantahala River valley.
3.9	Reach *Cold Spring Shelter* and *spring* on left.
5.2	Reach Burningtown Gap (4,236 ft.). Gravel road (N.C. 1397) to Kyle is on right. A.T. is graded trail crossing area, bearing right to woods.
6.1	Cross ridge with logging roads. Continue on graded trail.
7.6	Reach Licklog Gap, a clearing with *campsites* and a logging road on right.
9.2	Start climb toward Wayah Bald.
9.4	Reach *campsite* with *spring* on right.
9.6	Cross woods road. The Bartram Trail (marked with yellow blazes) comes in from left. Both trails (the Bartram and A.T.) are the same over Wayah Bald.
9.8	Reach crest of Wayah Bald (5,336 ft.) The A.T. (and Bartram Trail) crosses the summit and descends S slope by a macadam path.
10.0	A.T. and Bartram Trail bear R above parking area; latrine is on R at trail jct.
10.2	Cross woods road with log steps.
11.5	Come to logging road on right.
11.7	Reach *Wine Spring* and *campsite* on right.
11.8	Bartram Trail leaves A.T. and bears right on McDonald Ridge.
12.0	Cross USFS gravel road. There is a piped *spring* on left, beside the steps. The A.T. parallels the road for the next 2 mi.
14.1	Cross N.C. 1310 in Wayah Gap (4,180 ft.) at log steps. The Wayah Crest picnic area is 500 ft. to right at road crossing.

Trail Description, South to North

Miles	Data
0.0	Northbound A.T. starts at the log steps in Wayah Gap (4,180 ft.), on right of USFS gravel road to Wayah Bald, and parallels road for 2 mi.
2.0	Cross road. There is a piped *spring* on right of log steps.
2.3	Reach junction with Bartram Trail (marked with yellow blazes) which comes in from McDonald Ridge on left.
2.4	Reach *Wine Spring* and campsite on left.
2.6	Reach logging road to Wine Spring Bald, on right.
3.9	Cross woods road with log steps.
4.1	Reach jct. with macadam path; turn L toward observation tower. Latrine is on L. The A.T. and the Bartram Trail cross the tower area and descend N slope.
4.5	Cross woods road with log steps. The Bartram Trail turns right.
4.7	Reach *campsite* and *spring* on left. The slope is more gradual from here.
6.5	Reach Licklog Gap. There is a level area with *campsites* and a logging road on left.
8.0	Cross ridge with logging roads. The A.T. is a graded trail across this area.
8.6	Reach *stream* with log bridge.
8.9	Come into Burningtown Gap (4,236 ft.). Gravel road (N.C. 1397) from Kyle comes in on left. Cross area and start to climb toward Burningtown Bald by graded trail.
10.2	Reach *Cold Spring Shelter* and *spring* on right.
10.6	Reach Copper Bald (5,200 ft.). The Trail is narrow and rocky from here, crossing in succession Tellico Bald, Black Bald, and Rocky Bald.
12.4	Reach *campsite* and *spring* on left. Start descent to Tellico Gap.
14.1	Reach Tellico Gap (3,850 ft.). Gravel road (N.C. 1365) from state highway is left of fireroad to Wesser Bald straight ahead. A.T. bears to left of fireroad.

SECTION 8

WAYAH GAP TO WALLACE GAP

Distance 9.1 Miles

Brief Description of Section

This section begins in Wayah Gap (4,180 ft.) where the A.T. crosses N.C. 1310. It climbs Siler Bald (5,216 ft.), follows the crest of the Nantahalas, crossing a series of knobs and gaps with moderate changes in grade and descends to Wallace Gap (3,738 ft.).

Points of Interest

The highest point on this section is Siler Bald (5,216 ft.) named for William Siler whose great-grandson, the Rev. A. Rufus Morgan, helped establish the A.T. in N.C.

Road Approaches

Wayah Gap is accessible by N.C. 1310 which links U.S. 19 and U.S.64. Franklin, N.C., is 16 mi. to E. Winding Stair Gap, 12 mi. W of Franklin, is also accessible from U.S. 64, the Trail crossing the road at that point. U.S. 64 leads 33 mi. W to Hayesville and Lake Chatuge.

Wallace Gap, the S end of this section, can be reached by "old 64" which is now a state highway.

Maps

USFS Nantahala National Forest map and the TVA Wayah Bald and Rainbow Springs quadrangles. (Recent relocations of the A.T. are not shown on these maps.)

Shelters, Campsites, and Water

Siler Bald Shelter is located on a blue-blazed, 0.5-mi. side trail, whose junction with the A.T. is 2.2 mi. S of Wayah Gap, and 6.9 mi. N of Wallace Gap.

There are trash cans at Winding Stair Gap and at Wayah Gap, in the Wayah Crest picnic area, 500 ft. W of the A.T. crossing on N.C. 1310.

Standing Indian Campground, a USFS facility with camping spaces and the only telephone on the Trail in N.C. S of Wesser, is located 1.5 mi. S of "old 64" in Wallace Gap.

There are several stream crossings on this section and two springs, one near Siler Bald Shelter, the other at the parking area in Winding Stair Gap.

Public Accommodations

U.S. 64 through Winding Stair Gap is the most direct route to Franklin, N.C. for motels, post office, outdoor equipment, groceries.

Trail Description, North to South

Miles	Data
0.0	A.T. southbound starts at highway crossing in Wayah Gap (4,180 ft.), skirts Wayah Crest picnic area, crosses logging road, and starts the ascent of Siler Bald along W slope.
1.6	Reach clearing, 100 ft. across, with logging roads on both sides. A.T. crosses clearing (blazes are often obscured by weeds) and enters woods by graded trail.
2.1	Make sharp left turn onto woods road at log steps.
2.2	Reach junction of *Siler Bald Shelter Trail*. A.T. bears right, downhill. The blue-blazed trail continues ahead for 500 ft., then turns left, 0.5 mi., to *Siler Bald Shelter*.
3.9	Reach Panther Gap, a level area with campsites.
4.8	Reach Swinging Lick Gap. Make sharp turn to left.
4.9	Cross *stream*. There are *campsites* on left.
5.9	Reach Winding Stair Gap. A.T. comes out on road bank, and crosses U.S. 64. Parking area and southbound A.T. are 500 ft. to right. There is a piped *spring* beside the steps leading S.
6.6	Cross *stream*.
8.3	Reach campsite on left at steps.
8.9	Cross *stream,* followed by steps.
9.1	Reach Wallace Gap (3,738 ft.). A.T. crosses "old 64" on left of road to Standing Indian Campground.

Trail Description, South to North

Miles	**Data**
0.0	In Wallace Gap (3,738 ft.), A.T. crosses "old 64" on right of road to the Standing Indian Campground and climbs road bank.
0.2	After series of log steps, A.T. crosses *stream* and turns left.
0.8	Reach campsite on right at log steps.
2.5	Cross *stream*.
3.1	Reach Winding Stair Gap. Descend to parking area (piped *spring* on left) and cross U.S. 64 approx. 500 ft. to right. Climb road bank before turning left into woods.
4.1	Come to *campsite* on right, then a *stream* crossing.
4.2	Reach Swinging Lick Gap. Make sharp turn to left, uphill.
5.2	Reach Panther Gap, a level area with campsites.
6.9	Reach junction of *Siler Bald Shelter Trail*. Bear left for 500 ft. at log steps. Make sharp turn right, uphill. Blue-blazed trail turns right for 500 ft., then left for 0.5 mi. to shelter.
7.5	Enter clearing with logging roads. Cross clearing, about 100 ft. across, and re-enter woods beside oak tree (blazed).
9.1	Skirt Wayah Crest picnic area and reach steps at highway in Wayah Gap (4,180 ft.)

WALLACE GAP TO DEEP GAP

Distance 21.8 Miles

Brief Description of Section

This section begins in Wallace Gap where the A.T. crosses "old 64". The Trail follows a long curving ridgecrest. The main feature is Standing Indian Mtn., part of the Blue Ridge range. Except for the S slope of Albert Mtn., the changes in grade are gradual. The A.T. circles Standing Indian Campground. USFS 67, the campground road, provides access to the Trail at several points. This is a long section of Trail and at least two days should be allowed for hiking it.

Points of Interest

Standing Indian Mtn. (5,498 ft.) provides a magnificent view of the Tallulah River gorge and the mountains in Georgia. Albert Mtn. (5,250 ft.) overlooks the watershed of the Little Tennessee River. Between these peaks the Trail provides views of Pickens Nose and Rabun Bald.

The A.T. skirts the edge of Wilderness S of Albert Mtn. The area as far as Deep Gap is in Wilderness.

Road Approaches

Wallace Gap can be reached from "old 64" which crosses the A.T. in the gap. "Old 64" leads to U.S. 64 W, then to Lake Chatuge and to Hayesville. U.S. 64 has been relocated in Winding Stair Gap, 3 mi. N, and hikers are advised to use this route when going to Franklin for supplies.

A gravel road, USFS 83, from Coweeta Hydrologic Laboratory near Otto, N.C., provides access to the A.T. at Mooney Gap. Deep Gap is reached only by a gravel road (USFS 71) which heads S from U.S. 64, 5 mi. W of Wallace Gap, just past the Clay-Macon Cty. line.

Maps

USFS maps of the Standing Indian Campground Trails, the Nantahala National Forest, and the TVA Rainbow Springs, Prentiss, and Dillard quadrangles.

Shelters, Campgrounds, and Water

There are four shelters on this section, all located near water. These are Rock Gap Shelter, Big Spring Shelter, Carter Gap Shelter, and Standing Indian Shelter.

At the S end, near Deep Gap, there is a picnic area with tables, latrines, trash cans and water about 100 ft. beyond tables. Standing Indian Campground, a USFS facility on the headwaters of the Nantahala River, is located 1.5 mi. S of Wallace Gap. It has camping spaces and the only telephone on the A.T. S of Wesser. There are also trash cans at Rock Gap.

Public Accommodations

Franklin, N.C., 16 mi. E of the relocation of U.S. 64 in Winding Stair Gap has motels, groceries, as well as the Wayah District Office of the Nantahala National Forest.

There are no public accommodations in Deep Gap.

Trail Description, North to South

Miles	Data
0.0	The A.T. starts at highway, "old 64", on left of macadam road, 1.5 mi. from Standing Indian Campground. A.T. parallels road for 0.5 mi.
0.6	Reach Rock Gap parking area. Side trail to John Wasilik Memorial Poplar is on left.
0.8	Reach the *Rock Gap Shelter*, about 150 ft. on right. There is *water* beside shelter. Climb steadily for almost 2 mi. (There are numerous shortcuts along the route which makes it necessary to mark the switchbacks with double blazes.)
3.2	Reach Glassmine Gap. (There is a blue-blazed Long Branch Trail on right. It is about 2.3 mi. to USFS 67.)
4.1	Cross *stream*.
6.0	Reach Big Spring Gap. A blue-blazed trail leads about 250 ft. on right to *Big Spring Shelter. Water* source is behind shelter.
6.3	Cross USFS 83, Ball Creek Road, a gravel road from Coweeta. A.T. bears left to summit of Albert Mtn.; a blue-blazed detour of the summit bears R, 0.7 mi.
6.5	Reach Albert Mtn. summit (5250 ft.). There is a firetower and magnificent view but no water. Descent of S slope is very steep and rocky.
6.8	Descend to USFS 83 in Bear Pen Gap. (Blue-blazed detour comes in on right. Bear left along road for 100 ft., then enter woods on left. ft., then enter woods on left.
7.2	Descend to road briefly, then climb to rock cliffs overlooking headwaters of the Little Tennessee River. The Trail passes the boundary of the Coweeta Hydrologic Laboratory.
7.8	Overlook.
7.9	At log steps, turn sharp right and cross culvert carrying water from *spring* above.
8.1	Reach Mooney Gap, a popular *camping site* with side trails. USFS 83 from Coweeta stops here.
9.0	Reach Betty's Creek Gap, a clearing and a popular camping site. Cross area by graded trail. (Woods road on right leads 0.5 mi. to USFS 67, 7 mi. S of the *Standing Indian Campground*.)

10.2	Reach vista, with views of Pickens Nose and Rabun Bald. Follow 4,800-ft. contour along Little Ridgepole Mtn. to junction with the Blue Ridge at Ridgepole Mtn. (5,050 ft.)
12.8	Reach Carter Gap, a large, level area with numerous *campsites*. *Carter Gap Shelter* is about 50 ft. from Trail on right. *Water* is 150 ft. downhill behind shelter.
13.6	Come to Timber Ridge Trail, which is blue-blazed, on right. This trail leads about 1.8 mi. to USFS 67 and trail to Big Laurel Falls.
14.2	Come to Coleman Gap.
14.8	Cross *stream*.
16.0	Reach Beech Gap, a clearing with side trails, *campsites,* and logging roads. *Water* source is about 100 ft. from Trail on left. (Blue-blazed logging road leads 0.8 mi. to Beech Gap Trail and Big Indian Horse Trail, both blue-blazed, both leading to USFS 67.) From Beech Gap, climb steadily to Standing Indian Mtn.
18.9	Reach Lower Ridge Trail, blue-blazed, on right, which leads about 3.5 mi. to *Standing Indian Campground.*
19.0	Enter rock-strewn woods road. (On left a trail leads, about 500 ft., to the summit of Standing Indian Mtn. On right, a blue-blazed trail leads about 500 ft. to *water.)*
20.2	A.T. changes to graded trail at steps.
21.0	Reach *Standing Indian Shelter,* on the right, beside a *stream.* (A recent relocation takes the Trail straight by the shelter on a graded trail.)
21.8	Reach Deep Gap at parking area. USFS 67 leads 7 mi. to U.S. 64. Deep Gap is a picnic area with trans cans, picnic tables, latrines. The blue-blazed Kimsey Creek Trail (3.5 mi. to Standing Indian Campground) begins on N side of picnic area.

Trail Description, South to North

Miles	Data
0.0	The A.T. enters Wilderness at Deep Gap. The Trail begins E of the parking area. Deep Gap is a USFS picnic area with trash cans, picnic tables, latrines. USFS 67 leads 7 mi. to U.S. 64 and the blue-blazed Kimsey Creek Trail.
0.8	Reach *Standing Indian Shelter,* on left of Trail beside *stream.* The A.T. is a graded trail past the shelter, straight ahead.
1.6	At log steps, enter rocky woods road.
2.8	Reach junction of 500-ft. trail to summit of Standing Indian Mtn. (5,498 ft.) on right. On left is a blue-blazed trail, about 500 ft. to *water.*
2.9	Reach Lower Ridge Trail, which is blue-blazed, on left; it leads about 3.5 mi. to the *Standing Indian Campground.*
5.8	Come to Beech Gap, a clearing with side trails, campsites, and a logging road. *Water* source is about 100 ft from Trail, on right. (A blue-blazed logging road on left leads 0.8 mi. to the Beech Gap Trail and the Big Indian Horse Trail, both blue-blazed, both leading to USFS 67.)
7.0	Cross *Stream.*
7.6	Reach Coleman Gap.
8.2	Reach Timber Ridge Trail on left, blue-blazed; it leads 1.8 mi. to USFS 67 and trail to Big Laurel Falls.
9.0	Reach Carter Gap, a large level area with *campsites.* The *Carter Gap Shelter* is 50 ft. from the Trail on left. *Water* is 150 ft. downhill beside the shelter. (The A.T. leaves the Blue Ridge at the base of Ridgepole Mtn., 5,050 ft., and follows the 4,800-ft. contour around Little Ridgepole to the junction of the Nantahala range.)
11.6	Reach vista, with views of Pickens Nose and Rabun Bald.
12.8	Reach Betty's Creek Gap. Cross area by graded trail. (Woods road on left leads 0.5 mi. to USFS 67, 7 mi. S of *Standing Indian Campground.*)
13.7	Reach Mooney Gap, a popular campsite with side trails. USFS 83 now stops here. Between Mooney Gap and Albert Mtn., the A.T. leaves Wilderness.
13.9	At log steps, cross culvert carrying water from *spring* above the Trail, and make sharp turn L. A.T. passes the boundary of

	the Coweeta Hydrologic Laboratory and skirts rock cliffs overlooking the watershed of the Little Tennessee River. The Trail descends to a gravel rd. for about 100 ft.
14.0	Reach overlook.
14.6	Descend briefly to road.
15.0	Reach Bear Pen Gap. Descend again to rd. About 100 ft. to R, begin the 0.3 mi. climb to summit of Albert Mtn. A blue-blazed detour of the summit trail continues up the rd. The blue-blazed Bear Pen Creek Trail, on L, leads 2 mi. to USFS 67.
15.3	Reach summit of Albert Mtn. (5,250 ft.) with firetower and magnificent views but no water. Descend along N slope on fireroad.
15.5	Cross end of USFS 83. Blue-blazed detour from summit comes in from L. Enter Big Spring Gap, a clearing with unmarked logging rds.
15.8	Reach *Big Spring Shelter*. A blue-blazed trail on left leads 250 ft. to shelter. *Water* source is behind shelter.
17.7	Cross *stream*
18.6	Reach Glassmine Gap. (The blue-blazed Long Branch Trail is on left, and leads 2.3 mi. to USFS 67.) Descend steadily for 2 miles. (Unmarked side trails and shortcuts along route make it necessary to mark switchbacks with double blazes.)
21.0	Reach *Rock Gap Shelter*, about 150 ft. from Trail on left. *Water* is beside shelter.
21.2	Reach Rock Gap and parking area. (On right, a 0.5-mi. side trail leads to the John Wasilik Memorial Poplar.)
21.8	Reach Wallace Gap. Cross "old 64". (Road to *Standing Indian Campground* is on left.)

DEEP GAP TO BLY GAP

Distance 7.1 Miles

Brief Description of Section

This section starts at Deep Gap in the Nantahala National Forest and follows the crest of the Blue Ridge, with views to the W of the Shooting Creek and Hiawassee River Valleys, and of Lake Chatuge. To the E are Standing Indian Mtn. (5,498 ft.), Big Laurel (5,100 ft.), and the Burton Reservoir. The Trail climbs steeply from Sassafras Gap on one side, and Bly Gap on the other, over Courthouse Bald.

Points of Interest

Bly Gap (3,840 ft.) with its open views NW to N.C.'s Tusquittee Range is an outstanding feature of this section, as are the views from the crest of the Blue Ridge.

From Deep Gap to the Bly Gap, the A.T. passes along the western edge of Wilderness.

Road Approaches

Deep Gap is accessible via a gravel road USFS 71, that heads S from U.S. 64, just past the Clay-Macon Cty. line, 5 mi. W of Wallace Gap, 6 mi. to Deep Gap.

Bly Gap may be reached from U.S. 76 through Dick's Creek Gap, 8 mi. S in Georgia. U.S. 76 connects U.S. 23 and U.S. 441 at Clayton, Ga. with Ga. 75 from Hiawassee, Ga. From Dick's Creek Gap, follow U.S. 76 for 2.8 mi. W and turn right, reaching Titus at 4.7 mi. Reach Blue Ridge Gap at 7.5 mi. At Blue Ridge Gap, it is 3.1 mi. N to Bly.

Bly Gap may be reached from U.S. 64 in N.C. Just beyond Shooting Creek Post Office, turn S on gravel road to Eagle Fork. Follow road for approx. 3 mi. Follow obscure road (hard to find) to right off main road about 2 mi. to Bly Gap.

Maps

USFS map of the Nantahala National Forest, the Standing Indian

Campground Trails, and the TVA Rainbow Springs and Hightower Bald quadrangles.

Shelters and Water

There is one shelter in this section, the Muskrat Creek Shelter, 3.9 mi. S of Deep Gap, 3.2 mi. N of Bly Gap. There is water at the Deep Gap and Bly Gap Camping sites.

Public Accommodations

There are no public accommodations in either Deep Gap or Bly Gap.

Trail Description, North to South

Miles	Data
0.0	A.T. enters woods on right of USFS 71, a gravel road. (The Deep Gap parking area is on the left of road. The picnic area and blue-blazed Kimsey Creek Trail are both on left, below road.)
1.0	Climb steeply to rock outcrop (blazes on rocks).
1.2	Cross *stream* on footbridge.
1.6	Reach ridgecrest, the highest point on route, along Yellow Mtn.
2.3	Reach Wateroak Gap.
3.1	Reach Chunky Gal Trail which is blue-blazed, on right. (This leads 5.5 mi. to U.S. 64.)
3.4	Reach Whiteoak Stamp, a grassy clearing.
3.9	Pass *Muskrat Creek Shelter,* 100 ft. from Trail on left. There is *water* and a latrine at site. Pass two *streams* in next mi.
5.2	Descend to Sassafras Gap.
5.6	Reach ridgecrest after steep climb.
6.3	Come to Courthouse Bald Gap woods.
7.1	Make sharp descent to Bly Gap, a large clearing with a *spring* on right, 100 ft. from edge of clearing. Woods road on left leads 0.5 mi. to campsite with *water*. (There are several, somewhat obscure, side trails leading E to Hightower Bald and W down Eagle Creek Fork of Shooting Creek.)

Trail Description, South to North

Miles	Data
0.0	From Bly Gap, proceed along narrow ridge and begin steep climb for the next mile.
0.8	Reach Courthouse Bald Gap in the woods.
1.5	Reach ridgecrest.
1.9	Come to Sassafras Gap, after sharp descent. A.T. crosses two *streams* in next mile.
3.2	After crossing two *streams*, come to *Muskrat Creek Shelter*, 100 ft. from the A.T. on right. There is *water* at site and a latrine.
3.7	Reach Whiteoak Stamp, a grassy clearing.
4.0	Reach Chunky Gal Trail, which is blue-blazed, on left; it leads 5.5 mi. to U.S. 64.
4.8	Reach Wateroak Gap.
5.5	Start descent from ridgecrest.
5.9	Cross *stream* on footbridge.
6.1	Reach rock outcrop (blazes on rocks). Descend sharply from here.
7.1	Enter Deep Gap at parking area. (USFS 71, a gravel road to U.S. 64, is on right. Picnic area and blue-blazed Kimsey Creek Trail to *Standing Indian Campground* are on left, below the road.)

Closed
Gentian

SIDE TRAILS IN THE NANTAHALAS

Side trails are an outstanding feature of this part of the Appalachian Trail. From Wesser on the Nantahala River to Bly Gap at the Georgia state line, there are at least 10 trails intersecting the A.T. Eight of the trails, which are in the Wayah District of the Nantahala National Forest, are maintained with the assistance of the Nantahala Hiking Club.

1. **WESSER CREEK TRAIL:** Blue-blazed, 12 miles round trip from highway bridge on U.S. 19 in Wesser.

Miles	Data
0.0	At bridge on U.S. 19, head E.
0.9	Reach Wesser Creek road, E of Wesser.
2.6	Reach end of road and beginning of graded trail.
3.0	Come to Wesser Creek and *shelter*.
4.3	Trail leaves creek, climbs toward Wesser Bald.
6.2	Reach junction with A.T. (Wesser Bald is 0.7 mi. S; bridge on U.S. 19 is 5.6 mi. N.) Follow A.T.
11.8	Reach A.T. crossing on U.S. 19.

2. **BARTRAM TRAIL:** Yellow-blazed, an 18-mile section of the Bartram Trail which intersects the A.T. near Wayah Bald.

Miles	Data
0.0	Leave trailhead on Wallace Branch (on N.C. 1315, 1.7 mi. from its junction with "Old 64" in the outskirts of Franklin, N.C., near the Wayah District Office).
1.3	Reach junction with old Trimont Trail from Franklin to Wayah Bald. Bartram Trail turns left.
10.0	Reach junction with A.T., 0.2 mi. N of Wayah Bald observation tower.
12.1	Bartram Trail leaves the A.T., and turns W on McDonald Ridge.
14.1	Bartram Trail reaches N.C. 1310, the state highway linking U.S. 19 and U.S. 64, 7 mi. W of Wayah Gap.

3. **JOHN WASILIK MEMORIAL POPLAR TRAIL:** Blue-blazed, 0.5 mi., easy.

Miles	Data
0.0	Start in Rock Gap parking area, 0.6 mi. from Wallace Gap on road to *Standing Indian Campground.*

4. **LONG BRANCH TRAIL:** Blue-blazed, 2.3 miles

Miles	Data
0.1	Trailhead is opposite the Back Country Information Center on USFS 67 in *Standing Indian Campground.*
1.5	Trail crosses clearing and turns onto woods road.
2.3	Reach A.T. in Glassmine Gap.

5. **BEAR PEN CREEK TRAIL:** At the time of publication, the trail is being re-routed due to local clearcutting.

6. **TIMBER RIDGE TRAIL:** Blue-blazed, 1.8 mi.

Miles	Data
0.0	Start in the Timber Ridge-Big Laurel Falls parking area, 5.5 miles S of the Back Country Information Center in *Standing Indian Campground.* Timber Ridge Trail bears left after crossing a log bridge.
1.8	Trail crosses Big Laurel Branch and climbs the ridge to intersect the A.T., 0.8 mi. S of *Carter Gap Shelter.*

7. **BEECH GAP TRAIL:** Blue-blazed, 2.8 mi.

Miles	Data
0.0	Start in the Beech Gap parking area on USFS 67, 5 mi. S of Back Country Information Center on a log bridge crossing.
0.5	Reach junction with Big Indian Horse Trail, also blue-blazed.
2.0	Reach junction with Big Indian Road. Beech Gap Trail turns left to follow road.
2.8	Reach A.T. in Beech Gap.

8. **LOWER RIDGE TRAIL:** Blue-blazed, strenuous, 3.5 mi.

Miles	Data
0.0	Trail starts at bridge across the Nantahala River in *Standing Indian Campground* and circles around the campground and then starts to climb by switchbacks to the ridge.
3.5	Reaches the A.T. 500 ft. N of the trail to the summit of Standing Indian Mtn.

9. **KIMSEY CREEK TRAIL:** Blue-blazed, 3.7 mi.

Miles	Data
0.0	Trail starts at bridge across the river in *Standing Indian Campground* and follows the Park Creek Trail along the river.
0.1	At woods road junction, Kimsey Creek Trail turns left.
0.7	Trail enters clearing, turns right to follow Kimsey Creek.
2.0	Reach log bridge crossing.
3.7	Enter picnic area in Deep Gap. The A.T. is beyond the picnic area, and crosses the gap at the parking area.

10. **CHUNKY GAL TRAIL:** Blue-blazed, a 5.5-mi. section of the Chunky Gal Trail that extends for 20 mi. through the Tusquittee District, strenuous.

Miles	Data
0.0	Trailhead is on U.S. 64, 16 mi. E of Hayesville, 7 mi. W of Wallace Gap.
5.5	Reach A.T. junction, 3.1 mi. S of Deep Gap, Deep Gap can be reached by USFS 71, 5 mi. W of Wallace Gap on U.S. 64.

THE A.T. IN THE CHATTAHOOCHEE NATIONAL FOREST, GEORGIA

(From the N.C.-Ga. State Line to Springer Mtn., Ga.)

Distance 77.5 Miles

Although north Georgia is partly within the southern coastal plain region, it offers numerous opportunities for both strenuous and long-distance hiking through a primitive wilderness area. The Appalachian Trail is mostly along ridges at elevations around 3,000 ft. Ascents and descents are sometimes steep. Scenic vistas are possible from many rocky overlooks along the Trail and from the summits of several of the loftier, and open, mountain peaks. From these vantage points as far as one can see extend the multiple mountain ranges of the southern Appalachians, gentle in contour and soft green in color.

North Georgia is Blue Ridge country. The mountains have the form of an enormous V, open to the N. The apex of the V is Springer Mtn., 3,782 ft. in height, the southern terminus of the more than 2,000-mile Appalachian Trail. Here the Blue Ridge, which enters Georgia just E of Rich Knob, reaches its southern extremity and swings back northward.

In the early years of the Appalachian Trail Conference, it was uncertain whether the A.T. should follow the eastern or the western arm of this V. The eastern arm was finally chosen because of its greater accessibility and the existence of a developed USFS trail system. Its selection necessitated, however, at the southwestern end of the Great Smokies, the crossing over from the range which is continuous with the western arm of the V. The route is via the Yellow Creek Mtns., Wauchecha and Cheoah Balds, and the Nantahala Mtns.

The confusing mountain system of the Southern Appalachians grows out of the forking of the Blue Ridge in southern Virginia, which, farther N, has been a narrow crestline ridge. In southern Virginia where the Roanoke River breaks through the range, the Blue Ridge forks. The eastern range takes a circuitous route far to the east. It is the watershed and contains many outstanding peaks, such as Grandfather, Whiteside, and Caesars Head, but it is inferior to the western range in elevation and general scenic interest. The loftier western range is crossed by several rivers rising in the Blue

Ridge and is broken into segments known, respectively, as the Stone, Iron, Unaka, Great Smoky, Unicoi, Frog, Ellijay, and Cohutta Mtns. The eastern and western ranges come together at Springer Mtn., in Georgia. Cross chains, enclosing beautiful elevated valleys, connect the two master ranges. From the forking of the Blue Ridge in Virginia, the A.T. follows the western range S through the Great Smokies, then utilizes one of the cross ranges, the Nantahala, to join the eastern range near the Georgia-North Carolina line.

Springer Mtn. is the southernmost limit of the Blue Ridge chain. Projecting south from Springer Mtn. is the Amicalola range terminating at Mt. Oglethorpe, the original southern terminus of the A.T. For the first 8.7 mi., this range is utilized for a blue-blazed Approach Trail between Amicalola Falls State Park and the A.T. on Springer Mtn.

Mt. Oglethorpe was an appropriate terminus when the A.T. was first blazed. However, during the 1950s and even earlier, private development and chicken farming intruded on the wilderness experience of the hiker. In 1958, the ATC, upon recommendation by the Georgia Appalachian Trail Club, decided to abandon Mt. Oglethorpe to development, and to move the southern terminus of the A.T. to Springer Mtn., well within, and protected by, the Chattahoochee National Forest. With this relocation and the continued efforts of the USFS, the entire A.T. in Georgia, including Springer Mtn., now lies within the boundaries of the Chattahoochee National Forest.

For the most part, the A.T. in Georgia was routed over a previously existing Forest Service trail along the Blue Ridge crest. The completion, in the spring of 1931, of a 20-mile link north of Tray Mtn., afforded the first continuous route from Mt. Oglethorpe, the original terminus, to the Great Smokies. Only relatively minor relocations since that time have changed the Trail from its original location.

In the 1960s the Georgia section of A.T. was threatened with almost total extinction by a proposed extension of the Blue Ridge Parkway from its end in North Carolina along the ridgecrest (and along the A.T.!) in Georgia to Kennesaw Mtn., outside Atlanta. Fortunately the road was never built. In 1968, by Act of Congress, the A.T. was designated one of the first two National Scenic Trails and was thereby given the maximum protection possible under the constraints of the multiple use concepts and practices of the U.S. Forest Service.

The Georgia mountains are aflame in April, May and June with flowering rhododendrons, mountain laurel and flame azaleas. A normally high annual rainfall insures lush vegetation, fields of ferns and wildflowers, and rushing, clear mountain streams throughout the summer in this section. The beauty of the southern forests with flowers and shrubs in full bloom leaves an indelible impression.

The Georgia section of the A.T. has 11 shelters. They are well situated at intervals permitting easy day hikes. All but one of these shelters are three-sided, open front types. All are floored and all have springs close by. The exception is the stone, two-room structure on top of Blood Mtn. It has four sides, a fireplace, shuttered windows, and a sleeping platform.

The A.T. and shelters along the Georgia A.T. are the management responsibility of the Georgia Appalachian Trail Club, Inc., a club of 260 members. Early members of the GATC helped to survey and construct the first locations of the A.T. in Georgia back in the 1920s and 1930s. Thus, the club has a rich heritage, and a long tradition of Trail stewardship, one that it has shared to varying degrees over the years with the USFS, Chattahoochee National Forest. GATC members may be seen most weekends, cutting weeds, removing blowdowns, painting blazes, installing water bars, building bridges, and, in general, improving the quality of the Trail and the hiking experience.

An ongoing project of the GATC, begun in 1978 and still in progress at time of publication, is the identification and signing of alternate, ''off-Trail,'' campsites. These are level, open camping areas near the Trail. Many have water sources nearby. These campsites are being identified in an effort to reduce the use of areas around shelters for camping. Many of the shelter areas over the years have been so overused that the soils are compacted and no longer support growth of grass and other ground covers. At the date of publication, five alternate campsites had been signed. These are described in this guide in the information covering the Trail section in which they are located.

Because volunteers do the work of Trail and shelter maintenance on the A.T., it is important that the hiking public help by not littering, by packing out what they pack in, by not abusing or vandalizing structures or signs, by not cutting across switchbacks which are there for a purpose, and by ''taking only photographs and leaving only footprints.'' Any hiker who might like to become involved in Trail maintenance or the activities of the club, is invited to contact the GATC and to participate in any of their Trail maintenance or other outings. (Write Georgia Appalachian Trail Club, Inc., P.O. Box 654, Atlanta, Ga. 30301).

For convenience, and use in this guidebook, the Georgia portion of the A.T. has been divided into the following sections, each accessible by car, except for the North Carolina-Georgia line and Springer Mtn.

Section 11: Bly Gap (N.C.-Ga. line) to Dicks Creek Gap
(U.S. 76) ....8.7 mi.
Section 12: Dicks Creek Gap (U.S. 76) to Unicoi Gap
(Ga. 75) ....16.6 mi.
Section 13: Unicoi Gap (Ga. 75) to Tesnatee Gap (Ga. 348) 14.9 mi.
Section 14: Tesnatee Gap (Ga. 348) to Neels Gap
(U.S. 19 and 129) ....5.7 mi.
Section 15: Neels Gap (U.S. 19 and 129) to Woody Gap
(Ga. 60) ....11.3 mi.
Section 16: Woody Gap (Ga. 60) to Hightower Gap ....12.1 mi.
Section 17: Hightower Gap to Springer Mtn. ....8.2 mi.
Approaches to Southern Terminus of the A.T. (8.7 mi.) and Loop Hiking in Georgia.

BLY GAP (N.C.-GA. LINE)
TO DICKS CREEK GAP (U.S. 76)

Distance 8.7 Miles

Brief Description of Section

This section is the northernmost section of the Georgia A.T. Here the Blue Ridge has a somewhat lower elevation than to the N and S. The route is a graded trail broken by three gaps, Blue Ridge Gap (3,020 ft.), Plumorchard Gap (3,090 ft.), and Cowart Gap (2,920 ft.).

The division between the Chattahoochee National Forest (Georgia) and the Nantahala National Forest (North Carolina) is at Bly Gap. The TVA Hightower Bald quadrangle indicates that Bly Gap is not on the Georgia-North Carolina line but is a short distance north and in North Carolina.

From Bly Gap (3,840 ft.), the Trail follows the crest with little change in elevation, then drops steeply to Blue Ridge Gap. This section of the A.T. now traverses an area which was Congressionally designated Wilderness in 1984. From Blue Ridge Gap, the Trail ascends As Knob (3,440 ft.) and descends to Plumorchard Gap. It climbs up Buzzard Knob (3,760 ft.), down to Cowart Gap and then to Dicks Creek Gap and U.S. 76 (2,675 ft.).

Points of Interest

The highlight of this section without question is Bly Gap with its open clearing, excellent campsites, and views. The mountain range (about 320°) is the Tusquitee. The road to the right, snaking out of the mountains and descending to the valley below, is U.S. 64 through Winding Stair Gap.

Along this entire section are splendid views to the N of the imposing Standing Indian Mtn. (5,490 ft.) as well as of the Nantahala Mountains, in North Carolina. The isolated peak of Hightower Bald (4,568 ft.) is conspicuous to the NW.

Road Approaches

Bly Gap is not accessible by car. It is 5.5 mi. N, via the A.T., to Deep Gap, N.C., and 3.1 mi. S to the impassable road in Blue Ridge Gap. The nearest approach by car is from U.S. 64 in N.C.

Just beyond (W to E) Shooting Creek Post Office, turn right (S) on graveled road up Eagle Fork. Follow road for about 3 mi. beyond which point it becomes impassable. It is 2 mi. from this point to Bly Gap.

Blue Ridge Gap, 3.1 mi. S of Bly Gap, is crossed by a narrow, rutted rd. (USFS 72) which is not passable by car within 1 mi. of the gap. Beyond this point the rd. becomes passable, then paved; it leads 7.5 mi. through Titus, Ga., to U.S. 76, 2.8 mi. W of Dicks Creek Gap.

Dicks Creek Gap, the S end of the section, is on U.S. 76, 18 mi. W of Clayton and 11 mi. E of Hiawassee, Ga.

Maps

TVA Hightower Bald quadrangle, USFS Chattahoochee National Forest Map, Blue Ridge Ranger District.

Shelters, Campsites, and Water

The only shelter on this section is the Plumorchard Shelter, located near Plumorchard Gap, 4.4 mi. S of Bly Gap.

Excellent campsites and water are located in Bly Gap. There is water at the Plumorchard Shelter as well as a second spring 0.1 mi. from the Trail to the W of Plumorchard Gap. There is water at Dicks Creek Gap in the picnic area.

A signed alternate, or "off Trail", campsite is located on this section, about 1.0 mi. N of Dicks Creek Gap on Little Bald Knob.

Public Accommodations and Supplies

No facilities are available in or near Bly Gap. The nearest highway is U.S. 64 in North Carolina which is 5 mi. from Bly Gap, 2 mi. by trail and 3 mi. by road.

There is no public transportation in Dicks Creek Gap. Nearest reliable sources of supplies are in Hiawassee (11 mi. W) or in Clayton, Ga. (18 mi. E).

Precautions

Several trails converge in Bly Gap and caution must be taken to follow the A.T. To the W is a 5-mi.-route down Eagle Fork of Shooting Creek; it begins as a worn woods road. Another trail, as indicated on the TVA Hightower Bald quadrangle, leads to Tate City on the Tallulah River via Fall Branch. An earlier trail, no longer discernible, led about 1.5 mi. to Hightower Bald (4,568 ft.).

Trail Description, North to South

Miles	Data
0.0	From crest in ridge in Bly Gap (3,840 ft.), turn sharp left. Descend steeply about 100 yd., then turn sharply right into woods on graded trail. Cross left side of Rich Knob (4,132 ft.).
0.6	Come onto crest of Rich Knob. Follow along crest, at first descending, then on level section.
1.2	Old roadbed from Charlies Creek comes in on left. About 50 yd. farther, in level section, pass faint trail to right leading 1 mi. to headwaters of Hightower Creek.
1.7	Begin skirting left side of Rocky Knob (3,480 ft.).
1.9	Reach Rich Cove Gap (3,400 ft.). Beyond, continue on wide trail crossing right side of Wheeler Knob (3,560 ft.).
2.5	Come onto ridgecrest. Beyond, descent is very steep.
3.1	Reach Blue Ridge Gap (3,020 ft.) and dirt road, impassable for automobiles. Cross road and climb right side of ridge.
3.7	Reach high point of As Knob (3,440 ft.). Beyond, cross two small knobs.
3.9	Descent is steep down left side of ridge.
4.4	Reach Plumorchard Gap (3,090 ft.). (To left or E trail leads 0.1 mi. to *Plumorchard Gap Shelter* built by USFS in 1959. There is *spring* at *shelter*. There is a second *spring* about 0.1 mi. from A.T. on trail to right, or W, from gap.) From Plumorchard Gap, ascend steeply along right slope. (This is steepest climb along this section.)
5.2	Reach crest of ridge. Beyond, skirt left side of ridge.
5.5	Come into Bull Gap (3,550 ft.). Beyond, cross left side of Buzzard Knob.
5.9	Begin descent. Cross back and forth while descending narrow ridgecrest. Descend steadily.
7.0	Reach Cowart Gap (2,920 ft.). (Here old, impassable road between Hightower Creek and Holden Branch crosses Trail.) Circle right side of ridgecrest. Ascend steeply.
7.2	Pass *stream* 5 ft. to right of Trail.
7.5	Cross crest of ridge. Beyond, descend steadily down left side of Little Bald Knob (3,440 ft.).
8.7	Descend through picnic area and reach Dicks Creek Gap (2,675 ft.) and U.S. 76. To continue on A.T., cross highway.

Trail Description, South to North

Miles	Data
0.0	From highway in Dicks Creek Gap (2,675 ft.), follow Trail through picnic area and ascend steadily along right side of Little Bald Knob. Reach ridgecrest.
0.5	Bear right from crest, skirting E side of Little Bald Knob (3,440 ft.).
1.0	Cross over spur (3,160 ft.) on SE side of knob, continuing to ascend.
1.3	Reach crest of ridge. Beyond, descend.
1.5	Pass small *stream* 5 yd. to left. Descend steeply.
1.7	Come into Cowart Gap (2,920 ft.). (This is designated Tom Cowart Gap on USFS map.) Here is abandoned crossroad. From Cowart Gap ascend steadily, skirting left side of ridgecrest.
2.1	Cross to right side of ridge with knob on left.
3.0	Cross right side of Buzzard Knob (3,760 ft.).
3.2	Come into Bull Gap (3,550 ft.). Beyond, skirt left, then right side of knob. Beyond, descend steadily.
4.4	Reach Plumorchard Gap (3,090 ft.). (This is mid-point of section. To right or E blue-blazed trail leads to *Plumorchard Gap Shelter*. There is another *spring* 0.1 mi. from A.T. on trail to left of gap. Beyond *shelter* trail leads down Plumorchard Creek about 3 mi. to road at Plumorchard Church. In Plumorchard Gap old trail to left or W leads about 0.1 mi. to *spring*, and beyond down Big John Creek to Pleasant Hill School at dirt road on Hightower Creek.) From Plumorchard Gap, enter pine forest and ascend steeply toward summit of As Knob.
4.8	Come onto crest of As Knob.
5.1	Reach high point of As Knob (3,440 ft.). Beyond, descend steeply.
5.6	Reach Blue Ridge Gap (3,020 ft.) and dirt road which is impassable for automobiles. Cross road and ascend steeply along crest.
6.2	Cross left side of Wheeler Knob (3,560 ft.)
6.3	Come onto crest of ridge at Rich Cove Gap (3,400 ft.).

Beyond, climb right side of Rocky Knob (3,480 ft.). Come onto ridgecrest and follow crest.

7.5   In level section pass faint trail on left which leads 1 mi. to headwaters of Hightower Creek. About 50 yd. farther pass old roadbed which leads to headwaters of Charlies Creek. (Along this section are views of Hightower Bald in fall and winter.)

8.1   Leave ridgecrest, skirting right side of Rich Knob. Come into clearing on SE slope of Bly Gap. Turn sharply, uphill.

8.7   Reach cleared crest of Bly Gap (3,840 ft.). (There are several trails in Bly Gap which may be confusing. The A.T. turns sharply to right and continues directly ahead, to NE, along crest of ridge. Just N of Bly Gap a USFS trail leads E down Fall Branch to Tate City. To S about 1.3 mi. is Hightower Bald. To W is route to highway down Eagle Fork of Shooting Creek at U.S. 64 near Shooting Creek Post Office in N.C.).

DICKS CREEK GAP (U.S. 76) TO UNICOI GAP (GA. 75)

Distance 16.6 Miles

Brief Description of Section

Most of the Trail is graded and, in sections, utilizes old forest roads. Hiking this section is not difficult although there are several long, steady climbs.

From Dicks Creek Gap (2,675 ft.), the Trail ascends Powell Mtn. (3,850 ft.) and Kelly Knob (4,276 ft.), then loses elevation through a series of ascents and descents until it reaches its lowest point (3,400 ft.) in "The Swag of the Blue Ridge". Beyond, the Trail ascends Tray Mtn. (4,430 ft.), descends to Indian Grave Gap (3,113 ft.), climbs Rocky Mtn. (4,017 ft.) before descending to Unicoi Gap (2,949 ft.).

Points of Interest

The major points of interest are Tray Mtn, (4,430 ft.) with a splendid viewpoint, and "The Swag of the Blue Ridge" (3,400 ft.) a long, broad ridgecrest with little change in elevation for over 3 mi.

In the 1960s when the entire Georgia section of the A.T. was threatened with extinction by a proposed extension of the Blue Ridge Parkway down the mountain range along the route of the A.T., the GATC battled doggedly for, and won, preservation of "The Swag of the Blue Ridge" because of its unique qualities. Since the 1968 passage of the National Trails System Act and the designation of the Appalachian Trail as the first National Scenic Trail, the entire Georgia section of the A.T., including the Swag, has been given protection from roads and other intrusions.

From the crest of Tray Mtn. (4,430 ft.) there are superb vistas to the S and SE. Directly S is Yonah Mtn. The isolated peak to the SE is Curruhee Mtn., near Toccoa, Ga. On a clear day from the summit looking slightly W of S, it is sometimes possible to see Stone Mtn., the granite monolith outside Atlanta, about 100 mi. away. Farther N on the Trail, one may obtain views of the Blue Ridge. Brasstown Bald, the highest peak in Ga., is the prominent peak to the NW (about 300°). Rabun Bald, the second highest peak, is to the NE (about 60°). The Nantahala range can be seen directly N in N.C.

Between Tray Gap and Indian Grave Gap is an area called the "cheese factory". This was the site of a remote mountain farm, operated by a transplanted New Englander in the early 19th century. For an interesting account of the old "cheese factory" and of "Trail Mtn." (Tray Mtn.), read Charles Lanman's *Letters from the Alleghany Mountains,* published in 1849.

Road Approaches

Dicks Creek Gap is located on U.S. 76, 18 mi. W of Clayton, Ga., and 11 mi. E of Hiawassee, Ga.

In Addis Gap, 5.4 mi. S of Dicks Creek Gap, a fireroad (USFS 26) leads E about 8 mi. to Ga. 197 at Wildcat Creek near Lake Burton. To the W of Addis Gap, the road, impassable by car near the gap, leads about 5 mi. to Ga. 75 N of Unicoi Gap.

In Tray Gap, an unpaved road (USFS Rd. 79) leads SE to join the Clarkesville-Lake Burton Road (Ga. 197). To the SW, it leads to Ga. 75, N of Helen. This road was an old circuit road connecting Helen, Ga., with Clarkesville by way of Tray Gap.

In Indian Grave Gap, an unpaved and rough road leads left (when hiking N to S) to the Tray Mtn. Road from Ga. 75, N of Helen to Tray Gap.

The S end of this section, Unicoi Gap, is located on Ga. 75, 9 mi. N of Helen, Ga.

Maps

TVA Tray Mtn., Osborne, and Hightower Bald quadrangles, the USFS Chattahoochee National Forest Map, and the USGS Dahlonega quadrangle.

Shelters, Campsites and Water

There are two shelters on this section. One at Addis Gap, 5.4 mi. S of Dicks Creek Gap, has four bunks, table, and fireplace. The second shelter, near the summit of Tray Mtn. (the Montray Shelter), is 10.7 mi. from the gap and has no bunks.

There are good sources of water adjacent to both shelters. In addition, several streams cross the Trail.

Good campsites are located throughout this section. In particular, there are two alternate camping areas which have been signed by the GATC. One is located a few hundred ft. S of the summit of Rocky Mtn., about 1.3

mi. N of Unicoi Gap; the second, is near Dicks Creek Gap, just S of Snake Mtn., near McClure Gap (distance not measured at time of publication).

At the site of the old ''cheese factory'' near the Tray Mtn. Road are good campsites and a spring.

Public Accommodations and Supplies

At the N end, in Dicks Creek Gap, it is 11 mi. W to Hiawassee and 18 mi. E to Clayton for supplies.

At the S end, Unicoi Gap, it is 8 mi. S to Robertstown and 9 mi. to Helen, Ga., for supplies.

No public transportation is available through either Dicks Creek Gap or Unicoi Gap.

Trail Description, North to South

Miles	Data
0.0	From U.S. 76 in Dicks Creek Gap (2,675 ft.) follow Trail S on old road. Turn left off road and ascend gradually. In first mile cross small *streams*. Pass to left (E) of Snake Mtn.
1.1	Reach Hooper Gap (3,050 ft.). (Trail to right or W leads from Hooper Gap along Swallow Creek to Lower Hightower Church at the Osborne settlement on U.S. 76.) From Hooper Gap, bear left ascending to crest of ridge. Cross left (E) side of ridge, ascending steadily for about 1 mi. Continue on more gradual slope along broad ridge top.
3.1	Reach top of Powell Mtn. (3,850 ft.). Descend along right (W) side of ridge, to left of Wolf Stake Knob, then crossing back to right side of ridge.
3.5	Come into Deep Gap (3,550 ft.). (Trail to left leads E to Lake Burton; to right, trail leads W to Swallow Creek, and beyond to U.S. 76. For emergency exit, it is nearer to a highway to follow A.T. back to Dicks Creek Gap, than to use either of these trails.) From Deep Gap, ascend steadily, passing to right of Double Spring Knob.
4.0	Cross to left side of ridge in shallow gap.
4.3	Reach top of Kelly Knob (4,276 ft.), highest peak between N.C. line and Tray Mtn. (There are views in fall and winter about 200 ft. to right of Trail.) Descend gradually along SW slope.

5.4   Come into Addis Gap (3,304 ft.). (To left or E, fireroad leads to *Addis Gap Shelter*, built by USFS in 1959 near abandoned homesite of Addis family. Good *spring* is nearby.) From Gap, begin moderate ascent along ridgecrest, soon swinging to right (W) side of ridge.

6.0   Return to ridgecrest and begin descent.

6.2   Cross Sassafras Gap (3,500 ft.) *(Spring* is about 150 yd. downhill to NE.) Swing around left (E) side of Round Top (3,923 ft.). (This is E peak of Dismal Mtn.)

7.3   Cross Blue Ridge Swag (3,400 ft.), lowest gap in the general area and termed "The Swag of the Blue Ridge." (For about 3 mi. Trail follows broad ridgecrest with little change in elevation.) Ascend.

8.7   Swing around right (W) side of Young Lick Knob (3,800 ft.).

9.1   Reach Steeltrap Gap (3,500 ft.).

9.6   Pass Wolfpen Gap (3,550 ft.). Cross knob (3,880 ft.) and descend.

10.2   Come into gap (3,760 ft.). Begin ascent of Tray Mtn., crossing left (E) side of ridge.

10.7   Reach junction of A.T. with blue-blazed trail which leads to *Montray (Tray Mtn.) Shelter* (built by USFS in 1971). *Spring* is about 0.1 mi. from *shelter* on blue-blazed trail.

11.2   Reach summit of Tray Mtn. (4,430 ft.) with excellent views in fall and winter. (This is an outstanding peak of the Georgia Blue Ridge.) Descend steeply by switchbacks.

11.9   Good viewpoint is 100 ft. to left of sharp right turn.

12.0   Come into Tray Mountain Road (USFS 79) in Tray Gap (3,847 ft.). Cross road and continue on Trail along ridge. (At 12.3 mi. there is rocky cliff overlook to left, with views in fall and winter). Descend gradually.

12.8   Reach gap. (To right is site of old "cheese factory." See *Points of Interest.* Farther right, about 50 yd., is Tray Mountain Road, good *campsites* and *spring.*) Descend through laurel and rhododendron thickets.

12.9   Cross Tray Mountain Road (USFS 79). Continue descent.

13.9   Come to unpaved road in Indian Grave Gap (3,113 ft.). (To right is blue-blazed trail, earlier location of A.T. which leads S and connects with present A.T. just N of Unicoi Gap. This

	blue-blazed trail and the A.T. provide an excellent one-day loop hike.)
14.8	Begin steep ascent of Rocky Mtn.
15.2	Reach crest of Rocky Mtn. (4,017 ft.). Descend.
15.7	Pass junction with side (blue-blazed) trail which leads back to Indian Grave Gap.
15.9	Cross *stream*.
16.6	Reach Unicoi Gap (2,949 ft.) and Ga. 75. To continue on A.T. cross highway.

Trail Description, South to North

Miles	**Data**
0.0	From highway in Unicoi Gap (2,949 ft.), continue E climbing steadily along left side of ridge. Pass rock slides.
0.7	Reach *stream* which crosses Trail. Continue climb.
0.9	Reach shoulder (3,600 ft.) of Rocky Mtn. Take right fork in Trail. (Blue-blazed trail to left was former location of A.T. It leads N and connects with present A.T. in Indian Grave Gap. This blue-blazed trail, together with the A.T., makes an excellent one-day loop hike.) To continue on Trail, climb steeply and steadily.
1.4	Reach crest of Rocky Mtn. (4,107 ft.). (From rocky ledge, about 100 ft. off Trail to right, are good views to S in fall and winter.) Continue along ridge, descending gradually.
1.8	Descend more steeply. Pass through saddle in about 0.2 mi. and continue descent on graded Trail.
2.7	Reach road in Indian Grave Gap (3,113 ft.). (To left down road is a blue-blazed trail, site of the old A.T., which leads S and connects with the present A.T. just N of Unicoi Gap. The blue-blazed trail together with the A.T., makes an excellent one-day loop hike.) Cross road and ascend gradually through rhododendron, laurel thickets, and beds of galax.
3.7	Cross Tray Mtn. Rd. (USFS 79). Continue to climb. (To left of Trail is site of old "cheese factory;" see *Points of Interest*. To left about 200 ft. is Tray Mtn. Rd. Nearby are good *campsites* and *spring*.) Continue to climb (Hickory Nut Ridge to right) and continue on ridge.

4.3   (Rocky cliff and overlook to right of Trail affords views in fall and winter.)

4.6   Reach road (USFS 79) in Tray Gap (3,847 ft.). Cross road and continue on Trail up mountain. (At left turn, about 0.1 mi. beyond gap is a good lookout point straight ahead.) Ascend steeply by switchbacks.

5.4   Reach summit of Tray Mtn. (4,430 ft.) with excellent views in summer and winter. Beyond, Trail is rough, rocky, and steep.

5.8   Reach blue-blazed trail to *Montray (Tray Mtn.) Shelter* (built by USFS in 1971; *spring* nearby).

7.0   Pass Wolfpen Gap (3,550 ft.).

7.5   Pass Steeltrap Gap (3,500 ft.).

7.9   Swing around left (W) side of Young Lick Knob (3,800 ft.). Continue along ridge.

8.6   Begin descent into Swag of the Blue Ridge.

9.3   Cross Blue Ridge Swag (3,400 ft.), lowest gap in the general area and termed "The Swag of the Blue Ridge."

10.2   Continue around right (E) side of Round Top (3,923 ft.). (This is E peak of Dismal Mtn.)

10.4   Come into Sassafras Gap (3,500 ft.). Follow W side of ridge. (Off Trail to right, or NE, is *spring* about 150 yd. downhill.) After rounding ridge, descend into gap.

11.2   Come into Addis Gap (3,304 ft.). (To right, or E, down fireroad about 0.3 mi. is *Addis Gap Shelter*, built by USFS in 1959, near abandoned homestead of Addis family. Good *spring* is nearby.) To continue on A.T. from Addis Gap, ascend over knoll to another gap and begin long climb up ridge to Kelly Knob.

12.3   Reach Kelly Knob (4,276 ft.), highest peak between Tray Mtn. and N.C. line. (There are views from a point several hundred yd. to left of Trail.) Descend right (E) side of ridge.

12.6   In shallow gap, cross to left (W) side of ridge. Pass to left of Double Spring Knob.

13.1   Descend into Deep Gap (3,550 ft.). (Trail which crosses here leads right or E to Lake Burton, to left or W to Swallow Creek, and beyond to U.S. 76. To reach nearest highway, continue on A.T. to Dicks Creek Gap rather than use either of these trails.) Continue straight ahead from Deep Gap, passing first to left of

13.5   ridge, then to right of Wolf Stake Knob. Follow crest of ridge. Reach broad top of Powell Mtn. (3,850 ft.). From top, descend down right (E) side of Powell Mtn. Beyond continue over several spurs. Descend.

15.5   After long descent, come into Hooper Gap (3,050 ft.). (Trail to left of Hooper Gap leads along Swallow Creek about 5 mi. to Lower Hightower Church at the Osborne settlement on U.S. 76.) From Hooper Gap, descend to right along old roadbed and continue on E side of ridge. Pass to right of Snake Mtn. and remains of *shelter*. Cross three small *streams* in last mile of descent.

16.6   Come into Dicks Creek Gap (2,675 ft.) and U.S 76. (In gap is located Georgia State Highway Dept. picnic area.) To continue on A.T., cross highway.

UNICOI GAP (GA. 75) TO TESNATEE GAP (GA. 348)

Distance 14.9 Miles

Brief Description of Section

Viewed N to S, the Blue Ridge turns NW, then S to form the upper rim of a huge bowl, enclosing the headwaters of the Chattahoochee River, water source for Atlanta, the capital of Georgia, and many other municipalities.

This section traverses broad ridge tops with overgrown mountain-top fields. It utilizes well-defined trails and short sections of abandoned fireroads. There are several long climbs with elevations varying from 2,949 ft. at Unicoi Gap to 4,045 ft. at Horsetrough Mtn.

From Unicoi Gap (2,949 ft.) the Trail makes a steep ascent over Blue Mtn. (4,025 ft.) in about 1.4 mi., then descends past Rocky Knob to Chattahoochee Gap (3,500 ft.). Beyond, the Trail swings S, skirts Horsetrough Mtn., and drops into Poplar Stamp Gap (3,350 ft.). It then follows an abandoned road to Low Gap (3,050 ft.) and continues up and down with elevations ranging from 3,650 ft. on Poor Mtn. to 3,150 ft. in Wide Gap. Here, the Trail turns W and descends to Wolfpen Stamp (3,600 ft.) and Hogpen Gap (3,450 ft.). It then climbs gradually over Wildcat Mtn. and descends to Tesnatee Gap (3,138 ft.) and Ga. 348.

Points of Interest

One site of interest is Chattahoochee Spring, headwaters of the Chattahoochee River and drinking water source for millions of residents. From Chattahoochee Gap, location of spring, a 5.3-mi. blue-blazed side trail leads around Jacks Knob to Brasstown (Enotah) Bald, highest mountain in Georgia.

The Trail in Tesnatee Gap is crossed by an old road, impassable by car, which is reputed to be one of the oldest in the region. It was once a toll road over the mountain before the Neels Gap (Frogtown Gap) highway was built near the end of the 19th century. Charles Lanman, in his *Letters from the Alleghany Mountains*, wrote of stopping overnight in April,

1848 at the cabin of a poor farmer in "Tesnatee Gap" when on an exploratory journey to "Track Rock" from Logan's Plantation near Dahlonega, Ga.

Up until 1966 this section had been the longest section of the A.T. in Georgia not crossed by a paved highway. That year, the Richard B. Russell Scenic Highway, Ga. 348, was built from Ga. 356, NW of Robertstown, about 15 mi. to Ga. 180.

Unicoi Gap was first crossed by an old Indian trail. Later it was the route for the first road built across the mountain range. It is now a major highway, Ga. 75. A spring which is the headwaters of the Hiawassee River, is located E of Ga. 75 and N of Unicoi Gap about 400 yards.

Road Approaches

Unicoi Gap, the N end of the section, is located on Ga. 75, about 9 mi. N of Cleveland, Ga. To the N of Unicoi Gap, it is 14 mi. to Hiawassee, Ga.

Low Gap, 9.6 mi. from Unicoi Gap, may be approached but not reached from Ga. 75, from Robertstown.

Hogpen Gap, 14 mi. S of Unicoi Gap, is crossed by Ga. 348 (the Richard B. Russell Scenic Highway), which extends approx. 15 mi. from Ga. 356 (NW of Robertstown, Ga.) to Ga. 180.

Tesnatee Gap, the S end of this section, is also crossed by Ga. 348, N of Hogpen Gap. (To reach Tesnatee Gap, go N on Ga. 75 in Robertstown, Ga., turn left across the Chattahoochee River bridge onto Ga. 356 and at 2.5 mi. turn right onto Ga. 348.) It is about 10.7 mi. from Robertstown to Tesnatee Gap.

Maps

TVA Cowrock, Jacks Gap, and Tray Mtn. quadrangles, the USFS Chattahoochee National Forest Map and the USGS Dahlonega quadrangle.

Shelters, Campsites, and Water

There are three shelters on this section of the A.T. They are the Rocky Knob Shelter, 2.8 mi. from Unicoi Gap; the Low Gap Shelter, 9.6 mi.; and the Whitley Gap Shelter, located 1.1 mi. down a blue-blazed side trail which intersects the A.T. about 0.2 mi. S of Hogpen Gap on Ga. 348.

Springs are located near the Rocky Knob Shelter as well as 0.1 mi. farther S off the Trail, at Chattahoochee Gap, at Low Gap near the Low Gap Shelter and near the Whitley Gap Shelter.

Public Accommodations and Supplies

There are no bus lines operating through either Unicoi Gap or Tesnatee Gap.

From Unicoi Gap, the nearest stores and supplies are in Robertstown, about 8 mi. S on Ga. 75. Helen, Ga., another 2 mi. S on Ga. 75, has motels, groceries, shops and post office.

Trail Description, North to South

Miles	Data
0.0	From highway in Unicoi Gap (2,949 ft.), climb log steps and ascend steep, rocky slope. At top of slope, turn right on well-defined Trail and continue to climb.
0.5	Pass large rock slide.
0.6	Pass small *spring* to right of Trail.
1.2	Reach cleared area.
1.4	Reach crest of Blue Mtn. (4,025 ft.). Descend along top of ridge, which becomes narrow and rocky. Cross over to N side.
2.1	Reach location of old side trail, no longer visible but still shown on topo maps. (This trail, which may be impassable, leads down Watkins Branch, about 2 mi. to Ga. 180 and Ga. 66.)
2.3	Pass *spring* on right.
2.6	Pass Henson Gap (3,550 ft.).
2.8	Reach *Rocky Knob Shelter.* (*Spring* is about 150 yd. below shelter; if dry, use *spring* 0.1 mi. ahead on Trail.)
2.9	(*Spring* is approx. 50 yd. to right of Trail, down rocky slope.) Continue around Rocky Knob (4,015 ft.). Pass several rock slides and continue through dense woods on N side of ridge.

3.9   Come into Red Clay Gap (3,450 ft.). (Obscure trail to right leads around Jacks Knob and converges with trail from Chattahoochee Gap to Jacks Gap.)

4.3   Turn right on abandoned fireroad. Follow abandoned road along S side of ridge.

4.5   Reach Chattahoochee Gap (3,500 ft.). *(Chattahoochee Spring,* which is source of Chattahoochee River, is about 125 yd. down steep blue-blazed trail to left. Blue-blazed trail entering gap from right, leads around Jacks Knob and out Hiawassee Ridge about 2 mi. to Jacks Gap on Ga. 180.) Continue on Trail along ridge with fireroad on left. Follow narrow ridge.

5.2   Join abandoned fireroad in gap.

5.4   Leave road and begin sharp climb to right for about 0.2 mi. to top of knoll. Descent is slightly to left.

5.7   Join old road in Cold Springs Gap (3,450 ft.). (There is no *spring* in gap.) Begin gradual downhill and uphill grades on old fireroad skirting left of Horsetrough Mtn. (4,045 ft.).

7.2   Begin steady uphill climb. In about 0.5 mi., descend.

8.2   Reach road in Poplar Stamp Gap (3,350 ft.). (Campsites in gap; *stream* crosses old rd. to L of gap, several hundred ft. down old rd.) Continue S along fireroad.

9.6   Reach Low Gap (3,050 ft.) and *shelter. (Spring* and *campsite* are about 100 yd. to left or E. Two old trails, which may be indistinct and impassable lead into the valley to right or W. These trails converge at Stink Creek and connect with an old road which leads out to Choestoe.) Follow Trail S up slope. Climb steadily.

10.4   Reach crest of Sheep Rock Top (3,575 ft.).

10.7   Enter woods and continue along sharp ridge. Descent is gradual.

11.3   Come into Wide Gap (3,150 ft.). (A trail, which may be obscure and impassable, comes in on right. It leads out to old Tesnatee Gap-Choestoe Road.) Beyond gap, ascend along narrow ridge.

11.7   Reach top of Poor Mtn. (3,650 ft.). Descend along W side of ridge,

12.2   Come into Sapling Gap (3,450 ft.). Continue on Trail, crossing to left side of ridge.

12.5	Pass to left of Strawberry Top (3,710 ft.).
13.1	Reach crest of ridge at White Oak Stamp. Continue along crest, passing to left of Wolf Pen Stamp (3,600 ft.).
14.0	Reach Hogpen Gap and Richard B. Russell Scenic Highway (Ga. 348). Cross highway and ascend side of Wildcat Mtn.
14.2	On top of ridge, come to sign and blue-blazed trail leading 1.1 mi. to *Whitley Gap Shelter* (built by USFS in 1974). (To reach *shelter*, follow blue-blazed trail, descending *steeply*, through laurel and rhododendron. About 0.3 mi. behind shelter is a box *spring*.) To continue on Trail follow ridge N for 0.1 mi. and begin descent.
14.4	Reach rock cliff with view of Cowrock Mtn. to W, and 1,200-ft. deep gorge of Town Creek between. Descent is steep.
14.9	Reach Tesnatee Gap and Ga. 348. To continue on Trail, cross parking area.

Trail Description, South to North

Miles	**Data**
0.0	From Tesnatee Gap (3,138 ft.), climb steeply up Wildcat Mtn. by switchbacks passing large boulders and rock outcroppings.
0.5	Reach top of steep ascent (3,700 ft.). Continue to right along ridge.
0.7	Reach sign and blue-blazed trail to *Whitley Gap Shelter*. (To reach *shelter*, follow blue-blazed trail 1.1 mi. along ridgetop through laurel and rhododendron. From ridgetop there are magnificent views in season. Descend *steeply* to *shelter*. About 0.3 mi. behind *shelter* is a box *spring*.) Begin gradual descent.
0.9	Reach Hogpen Gap (3,450 ft.) and Richard B. Russell Scenic Highway (Ga. 348). (There is off-road parking in gap.) To continue on Trail, cross highway, climb log steps, and enter woods. Follow crest of ridge, passing to right of Wolfpen Stamp (3,600 ft.).
1.8	Reach Whiteoak Stamp. Here Trail leaves ridgecrest, descending on right side of ridge.
2.4	Pass to right of Strawberry Top (3,710 ft.).
2.7	Come into Sapling Gap (3,450 ft.). Beyond, ascend.
3.0	Reach open top of Poor Mtn. (3,650 ft.). Continue along ridge.

3.6	Pass Wide Gap (3,150 ft.). (Here Chattahoochee Trail comes in on left; it may be impassable. This trail leads to old Tesnatee-Choestoe road.) Ascend ridge.
4.5	Pass crest of Sheep Rock Top (3,575 ft.). Enter woods and begin steep descent.
5.3	Reach Low Gap (3,050 ft.) and *shelter*. (*Spring* and *campsites* about 200 yd. to right or E.) Follow fireroad along right side of ridge with gradual climb.
5.4	*Stream* crosses under road.
6.7	Come into Poplar Stamp Gap (3,350 ft.) (Campsites in gap; old rd. to R leads several hundred ft. downhill to *stream* crossing.) Follow Trail on old road and climb for approx. 0.6 mi. skirting E side of Horsetrough Mtn. at about 3,500-ft. elevation.
7.3	Begin gradual descent with occasional uphill grades.
7.7	*Stream* crosses road.
8.9	*Stream* crosses road.
9.1	Reach Cold Springs Gap (3,450 ft.). (There is no *spring* here.) Bear left leaving remains of old road on right. Ascend.
9.2	Reach top of knoll and descend steeply along top of narrow ridge. Continue on ridge.
9.4	Trail joins old road.
9.9	Leave old road and ascend steeply.
10.3	Come into Chattahoochee Gap (3,500 ft.). (*Chattahoochee Spring*, source of Chattahoochee River, is about 125 yd. down steep slope on blue-blazed trail. In gap, blue-blazed trail straight ahead leads around Jacks Knob and out Hiawassee Ridge to Jacks Gap on Ga. 180 about 2.5 mi.) From Chattahoochee Gap continue to right along S side of ridge.
11.0	Reach Red Clay Gap (3,450 ft.) (Obscure trail, entering on left, leads past Jacks Knob and converges with trail from Chattahoochee Gap to Jacks Gap.) Continue through thick woods passing several slides. Swing around left side of Rocky Knob (4,015 ft.); keep to right and cross spur to reach *shelter*, avoiding course down ridge.
12.0	*Spring* is about 50 yd. to left of Trail down rocky slope.
12.1	Reach *Rocky Knob Shelter* (built by USFS in 1960.) (*Spring* is 150 yd. below *shelter*. If dry, use *spring* 0.1 mi. back on

Trail.) Beyond *shelter,* continue on N side of ridge.

12.3   Pass Henson Gap (3,550 ft.). (Gap named for man who was ambushed and killed here many years ago.) Beyond, follow N side of ridge. Ascent is gradual.

12.7   Pass *spring* on left.

12.8   Reach top of ridge. (Trail to left which may be impassable, leads down Watkins Branch about 2 mi. to Ga. 180 and 66.) Continue on Trail straight ahead (E) down ridge which becomes narrow and rocky with steep sides. Alternately descend and ascend.

13.5   Reach crest of Blue Mtn. (4,025 ft.). Beyond, follow N side of ridge and descend.

13.7   Reach cleared area where old road swings S along top of ridge. Turn left on less distinct Trail and continue SE descending.

14.5   Pass small *spring* about 50 yds. to left of Trail.

14.6   Pass large rock slide and begin steep descent.

14.9   Reach Unicoi Gap (2,949 ft.) and Ga. 75. (A *spring,* which is the source of Hiawassee River, is located E of highway and N of gap. To reach *spring,* go N from small parking area, following indistinct path downhill for about 400 yd.)

TESNATEE GAP (GA.348) TO NEELS GAP (U.S. 19 AND U.S. 129)

Distance 5.7 Miles

Brief Description of Section

The A.T. in this section generally follows broad, rocky, scrubby tops along a well-defined route. From N to S, from Tesnatee Gap (3,138 ft.), the Trail ascends Cowrock Mtn., (3,842 ft.), descends to Swaim Gap (3,450 ft.), then climbs over Levelland Mtn. (3,942 ft.) and finally drops to Neels Gap (3,125 ft.) and U.S. 19 and U.S. 129.

Points of Interest

There are several excellent viewpoints on this section, rock outcroppings on Cowrock Mtn. and Wolf Laurel Top, as well as Levelland Mtn. (in fall and winter). The view from Cowrock is especially magnificent. From the height of the mtn., one looks down into the gorge of Town Creek, formed by the N-S ridges of Cowrock Mtn. and Wildcat Mtn. to the E. The view to the SE from Cowrock Mtn. includes Yonah Mtn., with its unusual steep, rock face. To the N is Brasstown Bald with its tower and buildings.

Road Approaches

The N end of the section, Tesnatee Gap, is located on Ga. 348 (the Richard B. Russell Scenic Highway). To reach Tesnatee Gap, go N on Ga. 75 in Robertstown, Ga., turn left across the Chattahoochee River bridge onto Ga. 356 and, at 2.5 mi., turn right onto Ga. 348. It is 10 mi. from Robertstown to Hogpen Gap and 0.7 mi. farther to Tesnatee Gap.

The S end of the section, Neels Gap, is located on U.S. 19 and U.S. 129, 19 mi. N of Cleveland, Ga., and 22 mi. N of Dahlonega, Ga. Neels Gap is about 14 mi. S of Blairsville, Ga., and 3 mi. S of Vogel State Park.

Maps

For maps, see TVA Neels Gap and Cowrock quadrangles, USFS Chattahoochee National Forest Map, and USGS Dahlonega quadrangle.

Shelters, Campsites, and Water

There are no shelters on this section.

Water is available and is signed at Baggs Creek Gap, 0.8 mi. S from Tesnatee Gap, at Rock Spring Top, 2.5 mi. from Tesnatee Gap, and at Bull Gap, 4.6 mi. from Tesnatee Gap. All may be intermittent in dry weather.

Campsites are numerous. There are spaces on Cowrock Mtn., on Wolf Laurel Top, in Swaim Gap, and in Bull Gap in addition to other locations.

Public Accommodations and Supplies

There are no sources of supplies or public transportation in Tesnatee Gap.

In Neels Gap, at the Walasiyi Inn, there is a store with hiking and camping supplies. In addition, Dorothy and Jeff Hansen (managers at time of publication) offer car shuttles, showers and overnight facilities for hikers. Write Manager, Walasiyi Inn, Route 1, Box 97A-20, Blairsville, Ga. 30512.

Trail Description, North to South

Miles	Data
0.0	Climb steadily from Tesnatee Gap (3,138 ft.) on Trail.
0.3	Come into grassy gap (unnamed). Climb is steep on switch backs.
0.8	Reach top of Cowrock Mtn. (3,842 ft.). (To left of Trail ar two separate viewpoints.) Continue down ridgecrest. Cros Baggs Creek Gap (3,591 ft.). (Blue-blazed trail to right lead downhill to *water.*) Climb back up ridge. Continue on Tra through rocky, scrubby area. Climb is steep.
2.1	Reach Wolf Laurel Top (3,766 ft.). (To left of Trail is ope rock face with excellent views.) Descend.
2.3	Pass Corbin Horse Stamp. Continue along ridge. Pass Roc Spring Top (3,526 ft.) with *spring* to right of Trail, ai Turkeypen Mtn. (3,550 ft.).
3.5	Reach Swaim Gap (3,450 ft.). Ascent is steep up rocky slope
4.1	Cross open, rocky area. (In fall and winter there are excelle⌐ views on either side of Trail.)
4.4	Reach summit of Levelland Mtn. (3,942 ft.). Descend alon⌐ gentle slope.

4.6   Reach Bull Gap (3,644 ft.). (Blue-blazed trail to right leads downhill about 200 yd. to *spring.*) Continue gradual descent along N side of Burnt Ridge. Continue on Trail through archway of Walasiyi Inn. (There are no public accommodations but there is a store with hiker supplies.)

5.7   Reach Neels (Frogtown) Gap and U.S. 19 and U.S. 129. To continue on Trail, cross highway.

Trail Description, South to North

Miles   **Data**

0.0   From road in Neels Gap, go through archway of Walasiyi Inn and continue on graded Trail.

1.1   Reach Bull Gap (3,644 ft.). (Blue-blazed trail to *spring,* about 200 yd. downhill to left of Trail.)

1.3   Reach top of Levelland Mtn. (3,942 ft.).

1.6   Cross rocky open area. (In fall and winter there are excellent views.) Descend on rocky Trail.

2.2   Reach Swaim Gap (3,450 ft.). Continue along ridgecrest, passing Turkeypen Mtn. (3,550 ft.) and Rock Spring Top (3,526 ft.) *Spring* to left of Trail.

3.4   Reach Corbin Horse Stamp.

3.6   Reach Wolf Laurel Top (3,766 ft.) after steep climb up rocky, eroded Trail. (To right of Trail are excellent *campsites* and views toward Wildcat Ridge.) Continue through scrubby, rocky area, then descend to Baggs Creek Gap (3,591 ft.). (Blue-blazed trail to *spring* to left of Trail.) Climb ridge.

4.9   Reach top of Cowrock Mtn. (3,842 ft.). (To right of Trail at two sites are excellent views to E.) Descent is steep on switchbacks.

5.4   Reach grassy gap (unnamed). Bear right around knoll.

5.7   Descend to Tesnatee Gap (3,138 ft.) and the Richard B. Russell Scenic Highway (Ga. 348). To continue on Trail, cross parking area and enter woods to right.

NEELS GAP (U.S. 19 and U.S. 129) TO WOODY GAP (GA.60)

Distance 11.3 Miles

Brief Description of Section

This section of A.T. is a pleasant day's hike between two paved highways. Despite two long, steep climbs (N to S), the section is termed moderate. From Neels Gap (3,125 ft.), the Trail ascends gradually over a recent relocation by the GATC (1981), then more steeply by switchbacks, and then gradually on a 1979 relocation (GATC) through rock outcroppings to the top of Blood Mtn. (4,461 ft.), where there are spectacular views. This 2-mi. section is perhaps the most hiked section of the A.T. in Georgia.

The Trail descends to Slaughter Gap (3,800 ft.). Beyond, through short climbs and descents it gradually loses elevation, crossing and paralleling old logging roads, until the ascent of Big Cedar Mtn. (3,737 ft.), and the descent to Woody Gap (3,150 ft.).

Points of Interest

The outstanding features of this section are Blood Mtn. (4,461 ft.) and Big Cedar Mtn. (3,737 ft.). According to Indian legend, a battle fought on Blood Mtn. between the Cherokees and the Creeks was so fierce that the mountain ''ran red with blood.'' Lichenous plants covering its rocky slopes have a reddish hue.

The views from Blood Mtn. are spectacular and worthy of some detail. From the rock outcrop near the stone shelter on the summit, there are splendid views S. The A.T. is to the right, on the broad, flat ridge leading back to Springer Mtn. Just below the summit a rock face provides a spectacular panoramic vista. To the SW is Yonah Mtn., with its unusual, steep rock face. To the NE, across Neels Gap, is Levelland Mtn. To the NE is the crest of the Blue Ridge with Tray Mtn. in the distance (about 75°).

A stone, two-room shelter is located near the summit of Blood Mtn. It was built in the 1930s by the Civilian Conservation Corps and is listed on the National Register of Historic Places. It was refurbished with new roof, window shutters, concrete floor, and bunk platform in 1981 in a cooperative project between the GATC and the USFS. Unfortunately for hikers, the top of Blood Mtn. has no firewood or water. The nearest water source is at Slaughter Gap, 1 mi. S, and it is intermittent.

Big Cedar Mtn. (3,737 ft.), 1 mi. from Woody Gap, has excellent views to the S from its rock outcropping.

The Lake Winfield Scott Recreation Area can be reached by a 2.2-mi. blue-blazed trail from Slaughter Gap and a 1-mi. side trail from Jarrard Gap. This area is closed in winter but, in season, has swimming lake, rest rooms, picnic areas and water. Lake Winfield Scott is located on Ga. 180, about 22 mi. N of Dahlonega via Ga. 60.

Maps

TVA Neels Gap quadrangle, USFS Chattahoochee National Forest Map, and USGS Dahlonega quadrangle.

Shelters, Campsites and Water

There is a stone, two-room building on the summit of Blood Mtn. (described in section above). It is about 2.1 mi. from Neels Gap. The closest water source is at Slaughter Gap, about 1 mi. to the S, and it is intermittent.

Campsites are numerous on this section, especially between Bird Gap and Woody Gap.

There are several water sources along this section: at Flatrock Gap, on a blue-blazed trail; at Slaughter Gap; Slaughter Creek; just south of Jarrard Gap; between Henry and Miller Gaps; near Granny Top Mtn.; and in Woody Gap, about 200 yd. on woods road. There are several stream crossings.

Public Accommodations and Supplies

In Neels Gap, at the N end of the section, there is a store at the Walasiyi Inn with hiking and camping supplies. Dorothy and Jeff Hansen, managers at time of publication, offer showers, shuttle service and rooms for hikers. Write Manager, Walasiyi Inn, Route 1, Box 97A-20, Blairsville, Ga. 30512.

In Woody Gap, it is 1.6 mi. to Suches, Ga., and a store and Post Office.

Facilities at Lake Winfield Scott, 2.2 mi. from Slaughter Gap, are seasonal and limited. Write USFS, Brasstown Ranger District, Blairsville, Ga. 30512.

Cabins and a supply concession (in season) at Lake Trahlyta are located at Vogel State Park, about 3 mi. N of Neels Gap off U.S. 19 and U.S. 129. For information, write Superintendent, Vogel State Park, Blairsville, Ga. 30512.

There are no bus lines operating through Neels Gap or Woody Gap. Nearest possible taxi service to Neels Gap is at Blairsville, Ga., 14 mi. N.

Trail Description, North to South

Miles	Data
0.0	On W side of highway in Neels Gap (3,125 ft.) ascend on graded Trail.
1.0	Reach Flatrock Gap (3,452 ft.). (Balanced rock is on left of Trail just before gap. Blue-blazed trail to intermittent *spring* is to right of Trail.) Ascend, sometimes steeply, by switchbacks through rhododendron and rock outcroppings.
2.0	Reach exposed rock with panoramic vistas. (See Introduction to section.) Continue steep climb.
2.1	Reach open rocky summit of Blood Mtn. (4,461 ft.). (This is the highest point in Georgia on the A.T. and affords splendid views. Near summit is stone, two-room, *shelter* with sleeping platform (built in the 1930s by the Civilian Conservation Corps; refurbished in 1981 by GATC. There are no firewood and no water on summit.) Descend steeply.
2.3	Turn sharply left off old jeep road onto forest trail. Begin graduate descent of SW side of Blood Mtn.
3.2	Reach Slaughter Gap. (Several trails converge in gap. Straight ahead, blue-blazed trail leads about 2 mi. to Lake Winfield Scott. Blue-blazed trail to immediate right leads downhill to intermittent *spring.* Blue-blazed trail on right beyond trail to *spring* is the Duncan Ridge Trail, a USFS National Recreation Trail, constructed in the 1970s by GATC and USFS.) Turn sharp left to continue on A.T. Descend gradually.
3.5	Reach *stream* (headwaters of Slaughter Creek) which crosses Trail. Within 200 ft., cross second *stream* (same source).

3.9   Reach Bird Gap (3,650 ft.) (Flat area with good *campsites* but no *water*.)

4.2   Ascend to shoulder of Turkey Stamp Mtn. (3,770 ft.). Turn left downhill. Descend gradually.

4.8   Cross Horsebone Gap (3,450 ft.). Ascend to near top of Gaddis Mtn. (3,545 ft.), then descend steeply.

5.4   Reach dirt road in Jarrard Gap (3,250 ft.). (Road to right leads about 1 mi. to Lake Winfield Scott.) Continue steep uphill ascent on old road.

5.6   Intermittent *water* on left of Trail.

5.8   Reach crest of ridge, known as Burnett Field Mtn. (3,200 ft.) Continue on Trail which bears left and descends gradually.

6.7   Trail passes within about 200 ft. to left of Henry Gap (3,100 ft.). (Unpaved road from Henry Gap leads to Ga. 180 near Mt. Zion Church.) Continue along left side of ridge (Baker Mtn.).

7.5   Reach *stream* which crosses Trail. (*Spring* is to right of Trail.) Continue gradual descent.

7.8   Cross small *stream* and turn right on old woods road. (Note: exercise caution throughout this section as Trail criss-crosses old woods roads.)

8.2   Turn left off old road and continue uphill.

8.3   Turn left onto old road. (Note: Trail no longer passes through Miller Gap which is private property. A.T. now passes within about 200 yd. of it.) Ascend along right side of ridge.

9.3   At crest of ridge, turn right on another road and, 100 ft. farther, bear right again, leaving road. Follow steep ascent by switchbacks.

9.4   Pass to right of Granny Top Mtn. and continue ascent.

9.5   Turn right on old road.

9.8   Pass *spring* on right. Continue ascent.

10.3   Reach rocky face of Big Cedar Mtn. (3,737 ft.) with views to S. Descent is steep.

10.6   Reach Lunsford Gap (3,300 ft.) which is open with excellent *campsites* but no water. Beyond gap, ascend briefly, then descend gradually. Continue to edge of woods and picnic area.

11.3   Reach Ga. 60 in Woody Gap (3,150 ft.). (Woods road, barricaded in 1982, on immediate right leads about 200 yd. to excellent *spring*.) To continue on Trail, cross highway.

Trail Description, South to North

Miles	Data
0.0	From Ga. 60 in Woody Gap (3,150 ft.) go N through picnic area and enter woods. (Unpaved road to left, barricaded in 1982, leads about 200 yd. to excellent *spring*.) Climb gradually along left side of ridge, then traverse crest.
0.7	Descend into Lunsford Gap. Beyond, ascent is steep.
1.0	Reach rocky overlook at top of Big Cedar Mtn. (3,737 ft.) with excellent views to S. Continue ascent to point where Trail becomes level.
1.5	Cross woods road diagonally and turn sharp left down ridge. In several hundred yd. pass *spring* to left. Bear right and continue, crossing several logging roads. (Trail passes to left of Granny Top Mtn.) At bottom of steep switchback descent, turn left onto old woods road. Within 100 ft. turn left again onto old logging road. Follow road downhill.
2.6	Turn right uphill leaving old logging road.
2.7	Come into woods road and ascend to right.
2.8	Turn off woods road and within 0.1 mi. come back onto road. (Note: Use caution throughout this section as Trail crosses and recrosses old logging roads.)
3.1	Turn left off road and cross small *stream*. Ascent is gradual. Baker Mtn. rises steeply on left.
4.1	Pass within about 200 ft. to right of Henry Gap (3,100 ft.). (Unpaved road from Henry Gap leads to Ga. 180 near Mt. Zion Church.) Ascent is gradual. Reach ridge and bear right.
5.3	Pass over flat area known as Burnett Field Mtn. (3,487 ft.)
5.5	Begin descent.
5.7	Pass intermittent *spring* in bank to right of Trail.
5.9	Cross dirt road in Jarrard Gap (3,250 ft.). (Road to left, USFS 34, leads about 1 mi. to Lake Winfield Scott.) Beyond Jarrard Gap ascent is steep.
6.3	Reach top of Gaddis Mtn. (3,545 ft.). Descend and bear right. Come into Horsebone Gap (3,450 ft.). Climb is steep.
7.1	Come onto shoulder of Turkey Stamp Mtn. (3,770 ft.).
7.4	Reach Bird Gap (3,650 ft.).
7.8	Cross *stream* (headwaters of Slaughter Creek). Within 200 ft., cross second *stream* (same source).

8.1   Come into Slaughter Gap (3,800 ft.). (In gap is jct. of several trails. Blue-blazed trail to L leads about 2 mi. to Lake Winfield Scott where blue-blazed trail straight ahead leads downhill about 200 ft. to intermittent *water*. Between these trails is a third blue-blazed trail, the Duncan Ridge National Recreation Trail, which leads to Ga. 180 at Wolf Pen Gap.) To continue on A.T. turn sharply to the R and ascend SW side of Blood Mtn.

9.0   Make sharp right turn and ascend on rocky old jeep road to summit.

9.2   Reach summit of Blood Mtn. (4,461 ft.). (This is the highest point on the Georgia section of the A.T. There are views in all directions of the Blue Ridge Mtns. Near summit is stone two-room *shelter* built in the 1930s by the Civilian Conservation Corps and refurbished in 1981 by GATC. There is no water at the summit.) Descent is steep.

9.3   Come out onto rock outcropping which affords excellent views (see introduction to section). Continue descent through rocks and rhododentrons.

10.3   Reach Flatrock Gap (3,452 ft.). (Blue-blazed trail to left leads about 200 ft. to *water*. Balanced rock is to right of Trail about 100 ft. from Gap.) Continue on graded Trail.

11.3   Reach U.S. 19 and U.S. 129 in Neels (Frogtown) Gap (3,125 ft.).

WOODY GAP (GA. 60) TO HIGHTOWER GAP

Distance 12.1 Miles

Brief Description of Section

This is one of the most interesting sections along the Appalachian Trail in Georgia. Here the Blue Ridge is richly wooded and consists of long ridges, breaking gently to the north, more steeply to the south. The Trail follows graded trails and woods roads for the entire section.

N to S, the Trail skirts Black Mtn. on a contour and continues with little change in elevation to Gooch Gap and USFS 42 (the Cooper Gap-Suches Rd.). Beyond Gooch Gap, the Trail follows the crest of Horseshoe Ridge, then follows old abandoned logging roads through a deep valley known as Devil's Kitchen (2,500 ft.). It then climbs Justus Mtn. (3,224 ft.), and descends to Cooper Gap and USFS 42 (Cooper Gap-Suches Rd.). Beyond, the A.T. follows ridgecrests through the Blue Ridge Wildlife Management Area to Hightower Gap (2,854 ft.).

Points of Interest

Although not on the A.T., the outstanding peak on this section is Black Mtn. (3,742 ft.), near Woody Gap.

Road Approaches

The N end of this section is on Ga. 60 at Woody Gap, about 5.6 mi. N of Stone Pile Gap, the junction of Ga. 60 and U.S. 19, and 15 mi. north of Dahlonega, Ga., on U.S. 19.

The south end, Hightower Gap, is located on USFS 42 (the Cooper Gap-Suches Rd.) The Trail crosses this road in three locations, Gooch Gap, Cooper Gap, and Hightower Gap.

This road is an all-weather road (unpaved) which terminates on Ga. 60 in Suches, Ga., about 1.6 mi. N of Woody Gap and 15 mi. N of Dahlonega, Ga. The distance from Suches to Hightower Gap is 12.7 mi.; to Cooper Gap, 8.4 mi.; and to Gooch Gap, 2.8 mi.

At the junction of roads (USFS 42 and 80) in Cooper Gap (Hightower Gap to Suches direction), a right turn onto USFS 80 leads about 2.7 mi. to a paved highway and the U.S. Army Ranger Training Headquarters. Here, a left turn onto paved road leads about 9 mi. to U.S. 19 just north of Dahlonega, Ga.

Maps

TVA Noontootla and Suches quadrangles, USFS Chattahoochee National Forest Map, and USGS Ellijay and Dahlonega quadrangles.

Shelters, Campsites, and Water

There is one shelter on this section, the Gooch Gap Shelter, located just off the Trail on a blue-blazed side trail, about 3.6 mi. from Woody Gap and 0.2 mi. from Gooch Gap (N to S). There is a spring approx. 0.2 mi. S of shelter. A second spring is located about 200 yd. before Gooch Gap (N to S), off the Trail, on a blue-blazed trail. Between Gooch Gap and Cooper Gap, there are several streams.

Public Accommodations and Supplies

There are no public accommodations at either end of this section of A.T. At the junction of Ga. 60 and USFS 42 (about 1.6 mi. north of Woody Gap on Ga. 60) in Suches, Ga., a store and Post Office.

There is no public transportation operating through Woody Gap.

Precautions

As noted in several locations in this book, hikers should exercise caution. November and December are deer hunting season in the Blue Ridge Wildlife Management Area.

The Army Rangers use this section, as well as much of the Chattahoochee National Forest, for training maneuvers. Hikers may encounter soldiers in combat uniforms, booby traps, gunfire and other aspects of Army maneuvers. Army Rangers, however, are under orders not to interfere with hikers.

Trail Description, North to South

Miles	Data ·
0.0	Cross highway (Ga. 60) into Woody Gap (3,150 ft.) passing through picnic area on W side of highway. Follow graded Trail along steep, heavily wooded, S side of Black Mtn.
1.1	Come into Tritt Gap (Side trail to right leads to Suches, Ga.) Take left fork.
1.3	Ascend steeply to rock ledge.
1.5	Reach crest of Ramrock Mtn. (3,200 ft.) with views to S. Descend by switchbacks.
1.6	Reach Jacks Gap (3,000 ft.). Beyond, ascent and descent are gradual.
2.3	Pass Liss Gap (2,952 ft.) which is overgrown with poplars. Bear right around N side of ridge.
2.6	Cross old abandoned and eroded road. Ascend and cross to left side of ridge.
3.0	Reach top of ridge and descend to Gooch Gap. (A few hundred yd. before Gooch Gap is blue-blazed trail on left to *spring.*)
3.5	Reach unpaved forest road (USFS 42) in Gooch Gap (2,784 ft.). (To right road leads about 2.7 mi. to Suches, Ga. where there are supplies and Post Office. To left, road leads 6.1 mi. to Cooper Gap.)
3.6	Reach blue-blazed side trail to *Gooch Gap Shelter* (built by USFS in 1959).
3.9	Descend on log steps. Pass *spring.* Ascend, bear L, then bear R around side of mountain.
4.7	Reach gap (2,950 ft.). Beyond gap bear right along crest of Horseshoe Ridge.
5.3	Bear left down side of ridge paralleling stream.
5.5	Reach mountain road. (To right road leads about 1 mi. past Mt. Airy Church to Suches-Cooper Gap Rd., USFS 42.) Turn left on road.
5.9	Cross Blackwell Creek on footbridge (built by GATC in 1981). Continue on abandoned logging road.
6.2	Several yd. to right is intermittent *spring.*
6.6	Cross Justus Creek on footbridge (built by GATC, 1981).
6.7	Cross old logging road. (To left on this road it is short distance

to Suches-Cooper Gap Rd., USFS 42). Begin ascent of Justus Mtn.

7.2   Cross over Phyllis Spur (3,081 ft.) and descend.

7.4   Reach saddle (2,900 ft.). Beyond, ascent is steep.

7.7   Reach top of Justus Mtn. (3,224 ft.). Turn left along ridge and begin descent by switchbacks.

8.3   Reach junction of forest roads in Cooper Gap (2,828 ft.). (Road downhill to left, is Cooper Gap Rd., USFS 80, and leads 14 mi. to Dahlonega, Ga. Road to sharp left, USFS 42, leads through Gooch Gap to Suches, Ga. Road ahead, USFS 42, leads to Hightower Gap. Road to immediate right, USFS 15, leads to the Gaddistown settlement). Cross USFS 42 and begin climb.

9.0   Climb to summit of Sassafras Mtn. (3,336 ft.). (Near summit and all along this section of the Chattahoochee National Forest, watch for Army rangers on manuevers.) Descend gradually.

9.9   Follow Trail through Horse Gap (2,673 ft.). (USFS 42 is visible to right; this is the Cooper Gap-Hightower Gap Road.)

11.7   Begin descent to Hightower Gap.

12.1   Reach road junction in Hightower Gap (2,854 ft.). (USFS 42 to immediate right leads back to Cooper Gap; straight ahead, it leads to Winding Stair Gap. USFS 69, between these two, leads about 2 mi. to Rock Creek Lake.)

Wild
Geranium

Trail Description, South to North

Miles	Data
0.0	From Hightower Gap (2,854 ft.) cross USFS 42 and enter woods.
0.4	Turn sharply uphill to right and follow ridgeline.
2.2	Reach Horse Gap (2,673 ft.) and continue steep ascent.
3.1	Reach summit of Sassafras Mtn. (3,336 ft.). (At summit as well as throughout this section of the Chattahoochee National Forest, watch for Army rangers training on manuevers.) Descend steeply.
3.8	Reach forest road junction in Cooper Gap (2,828 ft.). (Road to left leads back to Hightower Gap; road downhill to right, USFS 80, leads 14 mi. to Dahlonega. USFS 42 ahead leads through Gooch Gap to Suches, Ga., about 9.3 mi. Road to immediate left, USFS 15, leads to Gaddistown settlement.) Cross USFS 42 and enter woods to left of road. Begin steep ascent of Justus Mtn. by switchbacks.
4.2	Reach top of Justus Mtn. (3,224 ft.). Continue on ridge.
4.4	Turn right and descend to saddle.
4.7	Cross saddle and continue over Phyllis Spur (3,081 ft.). Follow switchbacks down mountain.
5.4	Reach old logging road (To right on this road it is a short distance to USFS 42.) Cross logging road onto another old road.
5.5	Cross Justus Creek on footbridge (built by GATC, 1981).
5.6	Pass road to right.
5.9	Turn right onto logging road. (Intermittent *spring* is several yd. straight ahead). Just beyond, bear left on abandoned road.
6.2	Cross Blackwell Creek on footbridge (built by GATC, 1981) and continue on old road.
6.6	Leave road, turning right on old trail which follows stream for short distance up mountain. (Road ahead leads about 1 mi. past Mt. Airy Church to Suches-Cooper Gap Rd., USFS 42.)
6.8	Reach top of Horseshoe Ridge and bear left along crest.
7.0	Reach peak of ridge (3,004 ft.). Follow crest of ridge down other side.
7.4	Reach gap (2,950 ft.). Bear left around N side of Gooch Mtn. on level Trail.

7.9	Turn sharp left and descend.
8.1	Bear right on Trail and descend briefly.
8.2	Reach blue-blazed side trail to *Gooch Gap Shelter* (built by USFS, 1959).
8.4	Pass *Gooch Gap Shelter* (built by USFS, 1959).
8.5	Pass Gooch Gap (2,784 ft.). (To left, USFS 42 leads 2.7 mi. to Suches where there are supplies and Post Office. To right it is 6.1 mi. back to Cooper Gap.) Cross road and enter wooded area. (To right of Trail, about 200 yd. down a blue-blazed trail, is *spring.)* Continue along gradually ascending ridge. Bear left, then right around N side of ridge.
9.2	Cross old abandoned and eroded road.
9.5	Reach Liss Gap (2,952 ft.). Continue along ridge.
10.4	Reach Jacks Gap (3,000 ft.).
10.5	Reach top of Ramrock Mtn. (3,200 ft.) with views to S. Descent is steep. Continue on slight upgrade.
11.0	Reach intersection with old trail in Tritt Gap (3,050 ft.). (Trail to left leads to Suches, Ga.) Continue on Trail around S side of Black Mtn.
12.1	Reach Ga. 60 in Woody Gap (3,150 ft.).

Trout
Lily

HIGHTOWER GAP TO SPRINGER MOUNTAIN

Distance 8.2 Miles

Brief Description of Section

The Appalachian Trail begins, or ends, depending upon one's point of view, at Springer Mtn. Prior to 1958, the terminus was Mt. Oglethorpe, but commerical development necessitated the relocation to a site within the Chattahoochee National Forest.

This entire section is within the Blue Ridge Wildlife Management Area where hikers must exercise caution during deer hunting season (November-December). This section of the Chattahoochee National Forest is used by the U.S. Army as a training area. Hikers are cautioned to expect to encounter Army trainees on maneuvers in full uniform, booby traps, sound of gunfire, and other simulated battle conditions.

From N to S, beginning at Hightower Gap (2,854 ft.), the Trail ascends Hawk Mtn. but no longer crosses its overgrown summit. From here, it follows ridgecrests, descending alongside Long Creek to Three Forks, where three mountain streams converge to form Noontootla Creek. From Three Forks, the Trail follows an old abandoned road along Stover Creek through a magnificent stand of hemlocks believed by many to be the only virgin hemlocks between Georgia and the Great Smoky Mountains National Park. Determined efforts of the Georgia Appalachian Trail Club, with the cooperation of the Chattahoochee National Forest, have succeeded in designating the present route as the official A.T. and thus protecting the hemlocks.

From the hemlocks, the Trail leaves the old logging road and crosses Stover Creek, then ascends through rhododendron to the summit of Springer Mtn., the southern terminus of the entire 2,100-mile long Appalachian Trail.

Points of Interest

The outstanding features of this section are Springer Mtn., the southern terminus of the A.T., the stand of hemlocks along Stover Creek, the rushing mountain streams which converge in the area called Three Forks, and Long Creek Falls, just off the Trail about 0.9 mi. N of Three Forks. In addition, this section is profuse in mountain laurel and rhododendron which bloom in June and July.

On the summit of Springer Mtn. there is embedded in rock a bronze plaque of a hiker, with pack on his back, ascending a mountain. This plaque was made by a member of the GATC, using another GATC member as a model. It was installed on Springer Mtn. in 1959 by the GATC after the A.T. terminus was moved from Mt. Oglethorpe. (There are two other plaques, one in Neels Gap and one in Unicoi Gap, which were installed in the early days of the GATC.)

From the rock overlook on Springer Mtn. there is a panoramic view of the Blue Ridge as it crosses Rich Mtn., into the Cohutta Mountains, to the NW.

Road Approaches

The north end of this section is at Hightower Gap, at the junction of USFS 42 and USFS 69. USFS 42 is an all-weather road which can be reached most directly from Dahlonega, Ga., via the Cooper Gap Road (USFS 80). Drive N on U.S. 19 about 2.0 mi. from Dahlonega to sign, "Camp Frank D. Merrill". Turn left on paved road which ends about 10.4 mi. at the Ranger Camp. Here, turn sharp right uphill on graveled road (USFS 80) to Cooper Gap at about 14.8 mi. In Cooper Gap, turn sharp left and continue to Hightower Gap at 17.0 mi.

A longer all-weather road is by way of Woody Gap and Suches, Ga. Drive N from Dahlonega on U.S. 19 to junction with Ga. 60 at Stone Pile Gap, approx. 9.4 mi. Here, bear left on Ga. 60, cross mountain, and A.T. in Woody Gap, and descend to Suches, Ga. at 16.6 mi. Turn left at store on USFS 42, pass Gooch Gap and cross the A.T. at 19.4 mi. Reach Cooper Gap and another crossing of the A.T. at 25.5 mi. Continue straight through gap to Hightower Gap at 29.3 mi.

The southern end of the section, the summit of Springer Mtn., may be reached via two approaches from the S and one from the N. (For directions, see section, "Approaches to the Southern Terminus of the Appalachian Trail," which follows this chapter.

Maps

TVA Noontootla quadrangle, USFS Chattahoochee National Forest map, and the USGS Ellijay quadrangle.

Shelters, Campsites and Water

There are three shelters on this section of the A.T. One is located on the side of Hawk Mtn., about 0.5 mi. S of Hightower Gap. The second is the Stover Creek Shelter, about 6.4 mi. S of Hightower Gap and 1.7 mi. N of Springer Mtn. The third is the Springer Mtn. Shelter, located on the summit of Springer Mtn., about 300 yd. down a blue-blazed and signed side trail. All three shelters have designated water sources nearby.

Campsites along this entire section are numerous and excellent. There are places on Hawk Mtn., along Long Creek, on Rich Mtn., and on the wide, flat summit of Springer Mtn.

Public Accommodations

The N end of this section, Hightower Gap, is located off USFS 42. It is well within the Chattahoochee National Forest and has no public facilities. Springer Mtn., the southern end of the section and southern terminus of the entire A.T., is accessible only by foot.

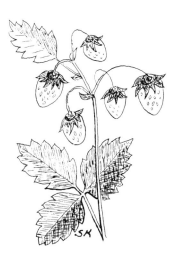

Trail Description, North to South

Miles	Data
0.0	Leave USFS 42 in Hightower Gap (2,854 ft.). Enter forest and ascend on graded trail, at first steeply.
0.5	Come to Hawk Mtn. Shelter. (Nearest water source is *stream,* 0.2 mi. S, on Trail.)
0.7	*Stream* crosses Trail. Continue on Trail along N side of Hawk Mtn. (Route over summit which is flat and overgrown, was abandoned in 1979.)
1.9	Reach USFS Register.
2.3	Reach graveled logging road. (To left, is Hickory Flats Cemetery Road. Pavilion at end of road may be visible from this point. Pavilion and picnic tables may be used by hikers.) Cross road and continue gradual descent on graded trail.
2.4	At this point, about 200 yd. to left uphill is the Hickory Flats Cemetery, a covered pavilion and a large cleared parking area which is the end of the Hickory Flats Cemetery Road. (This road leads back to USFS 58 near Three Forks.) Continue on gradual descent.
2.7	Trail turns sharp left onto old logging road. Caution: For next mile, pay attention to trail markings. In this section the A.T. and the Benton MacKaye Trail, blazed with an off-white diamond, are the same.
3.2	Reach sign and blue-blazed trail to right leading to Long Creek Falls, a spectacular water fall. Continue on Trail which parallels Long Creek.
4.1	Reach USFS 58 and area called Three Forks, the convergence of three mountain streams to form Noontootla Creek. (To left, road leads 2.6 mi. to Winding Stair Gap and USFS 42, which heads left to Hightower Gap.) Cross road and enter logging road to continue on A.T. (Road is gated to vehicular traffic.) In few hundred ft. cross Chester Creek.
4.6	Cross Stover Creek and turn left on Trail which follows old abandoned logging road and parallels Stover Creek. (For next 0.5-1.0 mi. observe the hemlocks, which may be a virgin stand.)
5.6	Turn left off logging road onto woods trail and descend,

crossing *stream* on log bridge. Ascend through woods on forest trails and logging roads.

5.7   Cross old logging rd. Stover Creek Shelter is approx. 200 ft. to R.

6.7   Reach ridgetop and junction with Benton MacKaye Trail (marked with off-white diamond).

7.0   Cross old logging road. (To left on logging road is *water* on a blue-blazed trail downhill. Benton MacKaye Trail leaves the A.T. at this junction. It rejoins A.T. on Springer Mtn.

7.2   Cross USFS 42. (To left, road leads 2.6 mi. to Winding Stair Gap and ahead to Hightower Gap.) Ascend through ferns and rocks.

7.9   Come to junction of A.T. with Benton MacKaye Trail. A few hundred ft. farther is blue-blazed side trail to left leading to Springer Mtn. Shelter and *spring*.

8.0   Reach sign and register.

8.2   Reach summit of Springer Mtn. (3,782 ft.) and junction of A.T. with blue-blazed Approach Trail from Amicalola Falls State Park. This is the terminus of the Appalachian Trail. (The rock overlook provides an excellent view of the Blue Ridge range as it crosses Rich Mtn., and heads to the Cohuttas in NW Ga. In the rock at the southern terminus of the A.T. is a bronze plaque of a hiker, with pack on his back, climbing a mountain. This was installed by the GATC in 1959).

Trail Description, South to North

Miles	Data
0.0	The A.T. begins at the summit of Springer Mtn. (3,782 ft.) at the junction with the blue-blazed Approach Trail from Amicalola Falls State Park. (To left at summit is overlook with excellent views of the western range of the Blue Ridge as it crosses Rich Mtn. and heads to the Cohutta Mtn. to NW. In rock is embedded a bronze plaque, approx. 14 in. by 16 in., depicting a hiker with pack on his back, climbing a mountain. This plaque was made by a member of the GATC and installed in 1959. Nearby on summit is sign and register.) Continue on Trail along flat summit.
0.2	Reach blue-blazed trail to *Springer Mtn. Shelter* (built in 1972) and *water*. A few hundred ft. beyond, reach junction of A. T. with Benton MacKaye Trail (marked with off-white diamonds). To continue on A.T. take left at junction of trails.
1.0	Reach USFS 42 (to right, road leads 2.6 mi. back to Winding Stair Gap and continues ahead to Hightower Gap.; to left, road leads to Doublehead Gap and to Ellijay). To continue on A.T., cross road and enter woods.
1.2	Reach old logging road; *water* is to right, downhill on a blue-blazed trail. Continue on Trail across logging road. (For next 0.3 mi. the A.T. and the Benton MacKaye Trail are the same. Pay attention to markings.) Ascend a shoulder of Rich Mtn.
1.5	Bear left to continue on A.T. (Benton MacKaye Trail continues ahead). Descend through woods on forest trails and old logging roads.
2.1	Reach *stream*.
2.5	Reach old logging rd. Stover Creek Shelter is located approx. 200 ft. to R on roadbed.
2.6	After crossing small stream on log bridge, ascend slightly and turn sharp right onto old logging road. (Within the next 0.5-1.0 mi., look at ancient hemlocks, which may be a virgin stand.) Continue on Trail along Stover Creek.
3.6	Make right turn and cross Stover Creek.
4.0	Cross Chester Creek on wide log bridge.
4.1	Reach USFS 58 and area called Three Forks, the convergence

of three mountain streams to form the Noontootla Creek. (To right, USFS 58 leads about 2.6 mi. back to Winding Stair Gap, and junction with USFS 42 which leads left back to Hightower Gap.) Cross road and continue on Trail up old abandoned logging road, barricaded to vehicular traffic about 300 yd. from USFS 58. This old road parallels Long Creek.)

5.0   Come to sign and blue-blazed trail to Long Creek Falls, a spectacular waterfall, to left of Trail. (Just beyond the trail to waterfall, the Benton MacKaye Trail turns left off old road while A.T. continues.)

5.5   Cross *stream* and observe double blazes. A.T. turns sharp right off old road, uphill through rhododendron thickets. (Caution: Trail and blazes are not obvious here.) Beyond the Trail climbs briefly, then continues on gentle slope. At one place, Trail recrosses old logging road.

5.8   Off Trail to right, several hundred yd. uphill, is the terminus of the Hickory Flats Cemetery Road which leads back to USFS 58. At end of road is large cleared parking area, covered pavilion with picnic tables which hikers may use. The Hickory Flats Cemetery is nearby.) Continue on Trail.

5.9   Reach graveled logging road. Cross road and continue on Trail.

6.3   Reach USFS Register.

7.0   Reach junction of old location of A.T. which once led over the summit of Hawk Mtn. (This route was abandoned in 1979.) Trail proceeds on N side of Hawk Mtn.

7.5   Cross *stream,* which is *water* source for *shelter*.

7.7   Come to *Hawk Mtn. Shelter*. Continue on Trail, descending gradually.

8.2   Descend into Hightower Gap (2,854 ft.) and junction of USFS 42 with 69. (USFS 42 leads ahead to Cooper Gap, Gooch Gap, and Suches; to right, road leads back to Winding Stair Gap. USFS 69, on immediate left, leads to Rock Creek. There are garbage cans in gap.) To continue on A.T., cross USFS 42 and enter woods.

APPROACHES TO THE SOUTHERN TERMINUS OF THE APPALACHIAN TRAIL

The southern terminus of the Appalachian Trail is at the summit marker on Springer Mtn. in Georgia. Since Springer Mtn. is the starting point for hundreds of northbound hikers each spring, and because the summit of Springer Mtn. is well within the Chattahoochee National Forest and accessible only by foot travel, detailed directions will be given in this section for the several most-used approaches to Springer Mtn. These include: 1). the approach to Springer Mtn. via Amicalola Falls State Park and the blue-blazed Approach Trail from the Park to the summit of Springer Mtn.; 2). a road approach to the blue-blazed Approach Trail via Nimblewill Gap where the Approach Trail crosses; and 3). a road approach to Springer Mtn. from the north via the A.T. For long-distance hikers, the approach to Springer Mtn. from Amicalola Falls State Park, although longer, may be preferable because of available parking and other facilities.

1. Approach to Springer Mtn. via Amicalola Falls State Park

General Information

Amicalola Falls State Park is located in Dawson County, about 15 mi. NW of Dawsonville, Ga. The falls for which the Park was named, are formed by the plunge of Amicalola Creek in several perpendicular cascades down the side of Amicalola Mtn., a distance of 500 ft. thus creating a spectacular "silver streak" on the mountainside which is visible from several points along the highways in this vicinity. The 406-acre Amicalola Falls State Park was established here in 1948, with picnic areas and grills. Today there are furnished cabins as well. Emergency shelter is available at the picnic area near the foot of the Falls. There is a telephone at the Park entrance. The Superintendent is Henry Johnson, Amicalola Falls State Park, Dawsonville, Ga. 30534. (Note: Park gates are opened at 7 a.m. and closed at 10 p.m.)

Amicalola Falls State Park is accessible by 1). Veterans Cab from Gainesville, Ga. (Gainesville can be reached from Atlanta's Trailways Bus Depot by American Coach Lines). 2). shuttle service from Dahlonega, Ga. (no bus service to Dahlonega from Atlanta). Two shuttle services in operation at time of publication are Fred Fritt, Route 2, Box 173A, Dahlonega, Ga. 30533 (404-865-6900) and Appalachian Adventures, Box

2057, Dahlonega, Ga. 30533 (404-864-7720). Arrangements should be made well in advance. It is about 27 mi. from Dahlonega to Amicalola Falls State Park.

Road Approach to Amicalola Falls State Park

From the square in Dawsonville, Ga., (about 13 mi. S of Dahlonega on Ga. 9) go N on Ga. 136. At 2.5 mi., at intersection with Ga. 136, bear left. At 9.4 mi. at intersection with Ga. 183, bear right. At 12.2 mi., turn right on Ga. 52. At 13.8 mi. at entrance of Amicalola Falls State Park, turn left.

Trail Description, Approach Trail to Springer Mtn. from Amicalola Falls State Park, South to North

Miles	Data
0.0	The blue-blazed Approach Trail to Springer Mtn. begins in the Park immediately behind the Visitors Center which is adjacent to the home of the Park Superintendent. (At the Visitors Center are rest rooms, vending machines and telephone.) Enter woods and ascend steeply along switchbacks.
0.8	Continue climb on road.
1.1	Turn right off road. (Trail to left leads to head of Amicalola Falls.)
1.4	Cross USFS road, climb steeply through laurel thickets to ridge top.
2.9	Cross abandoned road.
3.1	Reach Cemetery Road. (To left, road leads to old cemetery; to right, road leads about 2 mi. to Amicalola Falls-Frosty Mtn. Road, USFS 46.) Cross Cemetery Rd. and start ascent on forest trail, following the blue blazes.
3.8	Trail begins steep ascent of Frosty Mtn.
4.8	Reach site of old firetower and Frosty Mtn. Rd., USFS 46. (Wide, well worn trail to right leads to site of former shelter and *spring*. Summit of Frosty Mtn. is accessible, except in bad weather, by car via two routes: 1). via Amicalola Falls State Park, described above, and 2). via Nimblewill Gap, described below. It is 7.1 mi. farther from Dawsonville by way of Nimblewill Gap than by Amicalola Falls but the road is better.) To continue on Approach Trail, follow blazes into woods and descend.

5.1   At road junction, cross USFS Road. (Road to right leads 4 mi. to Amicalola Falls and 5.3 mi. to Ga. 52) Ascend and continue along ridge.

5.9   Reach Woody Knob (3,400 ft.). Descend steeply.

6.2   Reach road crossing in Nimblewill Gap (3,100 ft.) (USFS 28, to right leads 7.4 mi. to Nimblewill Church and 10 mi. to Ga. 52. USFS 46, down mountain to left, leads to Bucktown Settlement. Road sharp up mountain, leads 1.5 mi. back to Frosty Mtn.) Cross road in Nimblewill Gap and continue at first steeply, then more gradually up flat ridge.

7.0   Reach summit of Black Mtn. (3,600 ft.) (This is not to be confused with the Black Mtn. at Woody Gap.) Continue over Black Mtn. and descend.

7.3   Reach gap (3,400 ft.). (A campsite, signed by GATC, is located in this gap.) Follow flat ridge, then climb steeply.

8.7   Reach the A.T. on the summit of Springer Mtn. (3,782 ft.). Summit is flat and fairly wide. Here are registration cylinder, bronze plaque located on rock overlook, showing hiker facing north, and terminus marker. Bare rocky ledges afford excellent views of almost unbroken mountain range. This is an outstanding point in the Southern Appalachians. Here, join the two forks of the Blue Ridge which separate below Roanoke, Va. (For an account of the complex geographical structure of the Southern Appalachians, see "The Appalachian Mountain System" by Arnold Guyot, in American Journal of Science and Arts, vol. 31, second series, March, 1961, pp. 158-187.)

2. Road Approach to Blue-Blazed Approach Trail via Nimblewill Gap

This is the nearest road approach to Springer Mtn. via the blue-blazed Approach Trail from Amicalola Falls State Park. From Ga. 9, N of Dawsonville, turn left onto Ga. 52. At approx. 4 mi. turn right at old (perhaps unused) store. Continue past Nimblewill Church at 6.6 mi. Just beyond, pass road on left, where pavement ends. Continue to right on unpaved road. Reach Nimblewill Gap and the crossing of the Approach Trail at 14 mi. (To right, trail leads 2.3 mi. to the summit of Springer Mtn.;

to left, trail leads approx. 4.6 mi. back to Amicalola Falls State Park. To left, road leads 1.5 mi. to Frosty Mtn.)

3. Road Approach to Springer Mtn. via USFS 42 (Hightower Gap, Winding Stair Gap, and Big Stamp Gap)

From Hightower Gap (for directions, see Road Approaches, Section 16, Woody Gap to hightower Gap), follow USFS 42 to Winding Stair Gap at 3.9 mi. At Winding Stair Gap, first road to right (USFS 58), leads 3.1 mi. to Three Forks (name not shown on maps but is area where three streams converge to form the Noontootla Creek). Second road to right leads short distance only, to site of former Wildlife Ranger's cabin and *spring*. Road to left is Winding Stair Gap Road, USFS 58, steep and narrow, which leads 7.5 mi. to Nimblewill Church and 10 mi. to Ga. 52. Follow USFS 42 straight ahead 1 mi. to Big Stamp Gap and about 1.3 mi. to the crossing of the A.T. where there is an open field to the right (N) for parking. (To left, the A.T. leads about 0.9 mi. S to the summit of Springer Mtn.) (For detailed description of Trail, see Section 17, Hightower Gap to Springer Mtn.)

Great
Horned
Owl

LOOP HIKING IN GEORGIA

Springer Mountain to Slaughter Gap via Three Forks and Mulky Gap

Background

In 1978 with the building of a bridge over the Toccoa River, a 35-mile loop trail, under construction by the Georgia Appalachian Trail Club and the USFS, Chattahoochee National Forest, for more than a decade, was completed and designated "Loop Trail in Georgia." This trail forms a figure eight with the Appalachian Trail, leaving the A.T. on Springer Mtn., rejoining it and later leaving it in the Three Forks area, to rejoin it later at Slaughter Gap. This Loop Trail affords a variety of possible hikes, especially in conjunction with the A.T., the most challenging being a 65-mile circular hike bringing the hiker back to his point of origin. The trail description of this Loop Trail is detailed below.

In 1980, preparatory to assuming full management and maintenance responsibilities for the A.T. in Georgia, the GATC relinquished maintenance of the Loop Trail. The USFS, Chattahoochee National Forest, designated that section of the Loop Trail from Three Forks to Slaughter Gap as the Duncan Ridge National Recreation Trail. (At date of publication, the Duncan Ridge Trail has been given no distinctive marking.)

A newly formed trail association, the Benton MacKaye Trail Association, began in 1980, the construction of a hiking trail which, as originally planned, was to start on Springer Mtn., and proceed N to an area in Georgia E of the Cohuttas. From there the trail was planned to proceed along the ridgecrest of Tennessee-North Carolina to the Great Smoky Mountains National Park. The Benton MacKaye Trail was named for the founder of the A.T. and was originally planned along a route once considered for the route of the A.T.

At date of publication, the Benton MacKaye Trail Association has blazed with its off-white diamond marking, the route from Springer Mtn., via Big Stamp Gap, Three Forks, Ga. 60, to the top of Rhodes Mtn., most of this route having been the southernmost portion of the old Loop Trail. (From Rhodes Mtn., the newly constructed Benton MacKaye Trail leads W over Skeenah Gap, Wilscot Gap, Brawley Mtn., Garland Mtn, to the Shallowfords Bridge. This route has been constructed and blazed. Future plans are for the Benton MacKaye Trail to head generally W over Rich

Mtn. and N just E of the Cohutta Wilderness Area to the Georgia line. For information about this trail association and up-to-date information about progress on the trail, contact P.O. Box 53271, Atlanta, Ga. 30305.)

Despite the complexities of blazing and management responsibilities, the hiker is encouraged to hike "the loop." He will be guided in the section from Springer Mtn. to Rhodes Mtn. by off-white diamonds, and by blue, 2 by 6 in. blazes from Rhodes Mtn. to Slaughter Gap. The trail, regardless of blazing, is complete and has identified water sources. In general this trail is more difficult to hike than the A.T., has fewer water sources and is less maintained. However, it offers a challenging alternative to the A.T.

Trail Description, South to North

Miles	Data
0.0	The trail begins on Springer Mtn. (3,782 ft.) diverging to the right from the A.T. about 200 yd. N of the summit. It descends to USFS 42 near Big Stamp Gap. It then turns into the woods on old logging roads, and crosses streams.
3.2	The trail makes a sharp right turn onto the route of the A.T. which it follows for about 0.5 mi. as they both lead out over a shoulder of Rich Mtn. The A.T. turns left off the ridge while the Benton MacKaye Trail proceeds ahead, over the several peaks of Rich Mtn.
5.8	Reach area called Three Forks where three streams converge and USFS 58. Cross road and proceed to parallel Long Creek. About 0.9 mi. from the road is a sign to Long Creek Falls, a spectacular waterfalls. Trail continues, to turn left and cross stream (falls downstream). It then turns N following a tributary up a pleasant valley, then slabbing NW to a large clearing. Trail continues NW into woods and descends to gap (*spring* in draw to E). Trail then continues to N, with elevations ranging from 3,000-3,200 ft.
11.5	Trail descends to Bryson Gap (2,900 ft.) (*Spring* in draw to E). Trail then slabs W side of John Dick Mtn. (vista to W), descends to Sapling Gap, then follows long ridge NE to make gradual descent to river.

14.3   Reach Toccoa River and suspension bridge (completed in 1977 by USFS and GATC). Trail crosses river on bridge, makes steep ascent of Toonowee Mtn., followed by descent to Ga. 60 (2,028 ft.).

17.3   Reach Ga. 60 300 yd. W of Grizzle's Store and about 15 mi. W of Suches, Ga. Trail crosses Ga. 60 and Little Skeenah Creek and makes steep ascent of Wallalah Mtn. (3,100 ft.) with good views to S of summit. Here, trail turns W, descends 300 ft. before starting ascent of Licklog Mtn. (3,427 ft.). It then descends 300 ft. before climbing up and over Rhodes Mtn. (3,380 ft.). There is a *spring* to the R of trail between Licklog and Rhodes.

21.5   Reach summit of Rhodes Mtn. (Here, the route of the Benton MacKaye Trail, marked with off-white diamonds, leads W. From this point, the hiker should follow blue blazes to Slaughter Gap.) Continue along Duncan Ridge, passing Rhodes Mtn. Gap. Ascend 500 ft. to slab N side of Parke Knob, then drop into open meadow at Fish Gap (3,100 ft.).

25.2   Reach meadow in Fish Gap. (USFS 88 leads to USFS 4 which leads to Ga. 60.) From Fish Gap, trail slabs E around S side of Fish Knob with occasional vistas to S. After descent to Akin Gap (*spring* to SW), trail climbs Clements Mtn. (3,500 ft.) with vistas to NW and S.

28.2   Reach Mulky Gap (2,770 ft.). (In Mulky Gap, USFS 4 leads N to Highway 76 and S to Cooper Gap Scenic Area and Ga. 60.) Trail slabs S out of Mulky Gap, then turns E as it climbs Wildcat Knob (3,500 ft.) and continues over Buck Knob (vistas to E). It then drops into Bryant Gap (3,200 ft.).

30.2   Reach Bryant Gap. (This is the first of several points where the trail approaches but does not touch the Duncan Ridge Road, USFS 39, which turns from Mulky Gap and USFS 4 E to Wolfpen Gap and Ga. 180. *Water* is available at Bryant Gap by crossing road to S about 0.3 mi. and then dropping into draw to E.) Trail continues E on Duncan Ridge, climbing Buckeye Knob (3,820 ft.), descending to Whiteoak Stamp just N of Duncan Ridge Rd. (*water* across road about 200 yd. S down draw). Trail climbs Coosa Bald (4,271 ft.) which is the high-point of the trail (vistas to S). It then turns S to descend to

Wildcat Gap on the Duncan Ridge Rd. (3,770 ft.). It then slabs W side of Wildcat Knob close to the summit before a steep descent to Wolfpen Gap (3,300 ft.) and Ga. 180. There is *water* just off the far (S) side of Ga. 180 in Wolfpen Gap. (Wolfpen Gap is accessible by Ga. 180 from Vogel State Park and N from Lake Winfield Scott and Suches, Ga.) Trail crosses Ga. 180, enters woods, and climbs steadily reaching 4,150 ft. on E side of Slaughter Mtn. Trail then descends to its terminus in Slaughter Gap.

37.5 Reach Slaughter Gap and terminus of Loop Trail at A.T.

TOTAL LENGTH: 35.7 miles (total round-trip with A.T. to starting point is about 67 miles.)

SUMMARY OF DISTANCES

(Great Smoky Mountains National Park)

N to S (Read down)		S to N (read up)
0.0	Davenport Gap. Tenn. 32, N.C. 284	68.6
0.9	Davenport Gap Shelter	67.7
4.7	Mt. Cammerer	63.9
7.9	Cosby Knob Shelter	60.7
8.5	Cosby Knob	60.1
11.7	Maddron Bald Trail	56.9
13.5	Side Trail to Mt. Guyot	55.1
15.6	Tri-Corner Knob Shelter	53.0
16.5	Mt. Chapman	52.1
17.8	Mt. Sequoyah	50.8
20.5	Pecks Corner Shelter	48.1
21.8	Bradleys View	46.8
25.0	The Sawteeth	43.6
26.7	Charlies Bunion	41.9
27.9	Ice Water Spring Shelter	40.7
28.1	Boulevard Trail	40.5
30.8	Newfound Gap	37.8
32.4	Indian Gap	36.1
35.2	Mt. Collins Shelter	33.4
37.3	Mt. Love	31.3
38.3	Clingmans Dome	30.3
41.1	Double Springs Gap Shelter	27.5
42.4	Silers Bald	26.2
42.8	Silers Bald Shelter	25.8
45.1	Buckeye Gap	23.5
47.9	Sams Gap	20.7
48.2	Derrick Knob Shelter	20.4
49.2	Sugar Tree Gap	19.4
51.2	Mineral Gap	17.4
52.4	Thunderhead, East Peak	16.2
53.1	Rocky Top	15.5

54.2	Spence Field Shelter, Bote Mtn. Trail	14.4
56.6	Russell Field Shelter	12.0
57.4	Little Abrams Gap	11.2
58.8	Devils Tater Patch	9.8
58.9	Mollies Ridge Shelter	9.7
59.9	Ekaneetlee Gap	8.7
61.2	Doe Knob	7.4
63.4	Birch Spring Shelter	5.2
64.6	Shuckstack	4.0
68.6	Little Tennessee River, Fontana Dam	0.0

SUMMARY OF DISTANCES

(Nantahala National Forest and Chattahoochee National Forest: From Fontana Dam to Springer Mtn.)

N to S (read down)		S to N (read up)
0.0	Little Tennessee River	166.1
0.2	Fontana Dam Shelter	165.9
1.8	N.C. 28, Fontana Dam, N.C.	164.3
4.4	Walker Gap	161.7
5.9	Black Gum Gap	160.2
7.3	Cable Gap Shelter	158.8
8.1	Yellow Creek Gap	158.0
10.5	Cody Gap	155.6
11.3	Hogback Gap	154.8
13.0	Brown Fork Gap	153.1
14.7	Sweetwater Gap	151.4
15.7	Stecoah Gap	150.4
17.8	Simp Gap	148.3
18.0	Locust Cove Gap	148.1
21.0	Cheoah Bald	145.1
22.0	Sassafras Gap Trail Shelter	144.1
22.9	Swim Bald	143.2
25.9	Grassy Gap	140.2

84.9	Whiteoak Stamp	81.2
85.4	Muskrat Creek Shelter	80.7
86.7	Sassafras Gap	79.4
87.8	Courthouse Bald Gap	78.3
88.6	Bly Gap, N.C./Ga. State Line	77.5
89.2	Rich Knob	76.9
90.5	Rich Cove Gap	75.6
91.7	Blue Ridge Gap	74.4
92.3	As Knob	73.8
93.0	Plumorchard Gap Shelter	73.1
94.1	Bull Gap	72.0
95.6	Cowart Gap	70.5
97.3	Dicks Creek Gap, U.S. 76	68.8
98.4	Hooper Gap	67.7
100.4	Powell Mtn.	65.7
100.8	Deep Gap	65.3
101.6	Kelly Knob	64.5
102.7	Addis Gap Shelter	63.4
104.6	Blue Ridge Swag	61.5
108.0	Montray Shelter	58.1
108.5	Tray Mtn.	57.6
109.3	Tray Gap, Tray Mtn. Rd.	56.8
111.2	Indian Grave Gap	54.9
112.5	Rocky Mtn.	53.6
113.9	Unicoi Gap, Ga. 75	52.2
115.3	Blue Mtn.	50.8
116.7	Rocky Knob Shelter	49.4
117.8	Red Clay Gap	48.3
118.4	Chattahoochee Gap	47.7
119.6	Cold Springs Gap	46.5
122.1	Poplar Stamp Gap	44.0
123.5	Low Gap Shelter	42.6
124.3	Sheep Rock Top	41.8
125.2	Wide Gap	40.9
125.6	Poor Mtn.	40.5
127.0	White Oak Stamp	39.1
127.9	Hogpen Gap, Ga. 348	38.2
128.1	Whitley Gap Shelter	38.0
128.8	Tesnatee Gap, Ga. 348	37.3

129.6	Cowrock Mtn.	36.5
130.9	Wolf Laurel Top	35.2
131.1	Corbin Horse Stamp	35.0
132.3	Swaim Gap	33.8
133.2	Levelland Mtn.	32.9
133.4	Bull Gap	32.7
134.5	Neels Gap, U.S. 19 and 129	31.6
136.6	Blood Mtn., Blood Mtn. Shelter	29.5
137.7	Slaughter Gap	28.4
138.4	Bird Gap	27.7
139.9	Jarrard Gap	26.2
140.3	Burnett Field Mtn.	25.8
143.9	Granny Top Mtn.	22.2
144.8	Big Cedar Mtn.	21.3
145.1	Lunsford Gap	21.0
145.8	Woody Gap, Ga. 60, Suches, Ga.	20.3
147.3	Ramrock Mtn.	18.8
149.3	Gooch Gap	16.8
149.4	Gooch Gap Shelter	16.7
151.7	Blackwell Creek	14.4
152.4	Justus Creek	13.7
153.5	Justus Mtn.	13.6
154.1	Cooper Gap (Rd. Jct.)	12.0
154.8	Sassafras Mtn.	11.3
155.7	Horse Gap	10.4
157.9	Hightower Gap (Rd. Jct.)	8.2
158.4	Hawk Mtn. Shelter	7.7
159.8	USFS Register	6.3
160.3	Hickory Flats Cemetery	5.8
162.0	Three Forks, Chester Creek	4.1
162.5	Stover Creek	3.6
164.3	Stover Creek Shelter	1.8
165.1	USFS 42	1.0
165.9	Springer Mtn. Shelter	0.2
166.1	Springer Mtn.	0.0

INDEX

INDEX

INDEX

INDEX

INDEX

INDEX

INDEX

INDEX

INDEX

INDEX